Welcome to Wordmaster!

Liebe Schülerinnen, liebe Schüler,

sicherlich freut ihr euch darauf, Englisch zu lernen. Es ist spannend, wenn man immer mehr in der anderen Sprache ausdrücken kann. Klar, dazu muss man auch eine Menge Wörter lernen – und behalten. Und gerade das ist manchmal ganz schön schwer.

Wichtig ist aber nicht nur, dass man einzelne Wörter kennt, sondern dass man auch weiß, wie man sie richtig in Sätzen verwendet. Damit ihr Wörter besser lernen, ordnen, wiederholen und behalten könnt, wurde dieses Vokabel-Lernbuch geschrieben.

Der *Wordmaster* hilft euch, die neuen Wörter aus eurem Englischbuch mit Rätseln und spielerischen Aufgaben einfacher und besser einzuprägen. Ihr könnt auch malen und Karten basteln und einige Spiele zu zweit spielen. Ihr werdet sehen, so macht Wörter lernen Spaß!

Wordmaster ist mehr als nur ein „Vokabelheft", in das ihr die neuen Wörter eintragen müsst. Neben den vielen Übungen und Rätseln gibt es in jeder Unit einen besonderen Teil. Dieser Teil heißt *New words in combinations* und ist eng mit dem Wörterverzeichnis – dem *Vocabulary* – in eurem Schülerbuch verknüpft.

Bevor ihr die Lücken mit den neuen Wörtern ausfüllen könnt, habt ihr sie schon in der Schule und mithilfe des *Vocabulary* gelernt. Dann geht ihr zu den *New words in combinations* um euch selbst zu testen und zu lernen, wie man die neuen Wörter mit bereits gelernten Wörtern verbindet. Wie geht das? Ganz einfach: Für die neuen Wörter gibt es englische Beispielsätze und deutsche Entsprechungen. In den englischen Sätzen gibt es Lücken, in die ihr die passenden Wörter eintragen sollt. Die fett gedruckten Wörter in den deutschen Sätzen geben an, um welche Wörter es sich dabei handelt. Auf diese Weise schreibt ihr alle Wörter, die ihr im ersten Jahr lernt, nochmals in zusammenhängenden Sätzen auf. Hier ein Beispiel:

Bist du **neu**?	Are you _new_ ?
Ist Herr Braun **euer** Deutschlehrer?	Is Herr Braun _your_ German teacher?
Oh, **du bist** Sita. – **Ja**.	Oh, _____ Sita. – _____ .
Ashton ist **in der Nähe von** Chester.	Ashton is _____ Chester.

Die Reihenfolge bei *New words in combinations* ist übrigens die gleiche wie im *Vocabulary*, sodass ihr leicht dort nachsehen könnt.

Tipp: Wer gern mit Lernkarten arbeitet, sollte sich Kopien von den *New words in combinations* machen. Faltet die Kopien längs und klebt sie zusammen, sodass das Deutsche auf der einen und das Englische auf der anderen Seite steht. Schneidet die Streifen jeweils nach fünf Wörtern auseinander, dann habt ihr immer fünf Wörter auf einer Lernkarte. Stellt die Karten in eine Lernbox und ihr könnt jederzeit die Wörter wiederholen. Das ist wichtig fürs Behalten!

Noch ein Wort zu den Lösungen. Es gibt sie auf einem Extra-Lösungsschlüssel, der dem *Wordmaster* beigelegt ist. Allerdings solltet ihr die Lösungen nicht einfach abschreiben. Denn dadurch würdet ihr euch nicht nur um das Erfolgserlebnis bringen, selbst die richtigen Lösungen zu finden, sondern auch wenig dabei lernen. Ist die Übung oder das Rätsel gelöst, könnt ihr euch dann selbst überprüfen.

Ihr werdet sehen, wenn ihr den *Wordmaster* regelmäßig benutzt, vergrößert sich euer Wortschatz und ihr könnt euch einfacher und besser auf Englisch ausdrücken.

Ich wünsche euch viel Erfolg und Spaß beim Lernen!

Euer

Franz Vettel

A photo or picture of me

A photo or picture of my best friend/my favourite pet

My name is _____ .

I'm _____ years old.

I'm from _____ .

I'm in Form _____ at _____ School.

My address is _____ .

My telephone number is _____ .

This book is for the school year _____ .

1 Welcome! Hello, Form 7 CH!

▶ **Crossword puzzle**

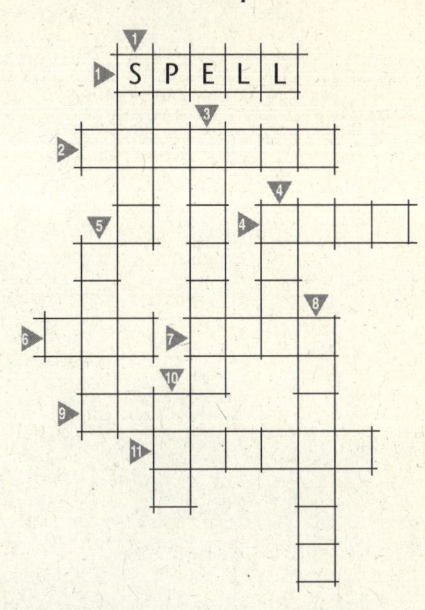

Across ▶

1 Can you … your name in English? – Yes, A-L-E-X.
2 I'm from Berlin. Berlin is in … .
4 How are you? – I'm …, thanks.
6 My dad is from Liverpool. My … is from Frankfurt.
7 I'm Alex. What's your …?
9 I'm German. Are you German, …?
11 Can you speak English? – Yes, a … .

Down ▶

1 I … German and a little English.
3 Good … . How are you?
4 I'm from Frankfurt. Where are you …?
5 Can you …? Yes – 1, 2, 3, 4, …
8 We speak … in the classroom.
10 I'm eleven. How … are you?

▶ **What colour is it? It's …**
Male das Bild aus.

1 = yellow • 2 = red • 3 = black
4 = pink (rosa) • 5 = brown (braun)
6 = green • 7 = blue • 8 = white

three

1. Hello, Form 7 CH!

▶ **New words in combinations 1/1** p. 12 – p. 16/A7

Ich bin in **Klasse** 5.	I'm in _____ 5.
Dies ist meine Englischlehrerin.	_____ my English teacher.
Sie ist aus Aachen, einer **Stadt** in Deutschland.	_____ from Aachen, a _____ in Germany.
Dies ist Jenny. Und dies ist **ihre** Schildkröte.	This is Jenny. And this is _____ tortoise.
Ist Sue deine **Schwester**?	Is Sue your _____?
Mike ist mein **Bruder**. **Er ist** zehn.	Mike is my _____. _____ ten.
Der Junge und das Mädchen sind **Zwillinge** –	The boy and the girl are _____ –
sie sind aus der Türkei.	_____ from Turkey.
Wie alt ist deine **Schildkröte**?	How old is your _____?
Frau Müller ist unsere neue Klassenlehrerin.	_____ Müller is our new form teacher.
Willkommen in Heidelberg.	_____ _____ Heidelberg.
Willkommen in der neuen **Schule**.	Welcome to the new _____.
Bist du **neu**?	Are you _____?
Ist Herr Braun **euer** Deutschlehrer?	Is Herr Braun _____ German teacher?
Oh, **Du bist** Sita. – **Ja**.	Oh, _____ Sita. – _____.
Ashton ist **in der Nähe von** Chester.	Ashton is _____ Chester.
Chester ist eine Stadt, **aber** Ashton ist ein **Dorf**.	Chester is a town, _____ Ashton is a _____.
Ich spreche **deutsch** und ein bisschen englisch.	I speak _____ and a little English.
Ben ist **nicht** aus Chester.	Ben is _____ from Chester.
Ben ist kein Deutscher, er ist **Brite**.	Ben is not German, he's _____.
Wie geht es dir? – Gut, **danke** (schön).	How are you? – I'm fine, _____ _____.
Sanjay ist ein **schöner** Name.	Sanjay is a _____ name.
Sanjay ist **Inder**.	Sanjay is _____.
Dies ist Sanjay. Sanjay ist mein **Freund**.	This is Sanjay. Sanjay is my _____.
Mama, dies ist Linda. **Wir sind** Freundinnen.	Mum, this is Linda. _____ friends.
Da habt ihr Glück.	_____ _____.
Tauschen wir – dein Lineal für meinen Kuli.	Let's _____ – your ruler for my biro.
Sehr witzig/komisch.	_____ _____.
Wo sind unsere Schultaschen? – **Hier**, …	Where are our school bags? – _____, …
… **unter** dem Tisch.	… _____ the table.
Die Tasche **öffnen**, bitte.	_____ the bag, please.
auf **Seite** 10	on _____ 10
Schlagt Seite 10 auf.	_____ your books ____ _____ 10.

1 ▶ Questions, questions
Verbinde die Wörter um Fragen zu bilden.

Hello. What's —— your name?
Where —— or English?
Are you two —— your name?
What colour —— near Chester?
Is Ashton a village —— friends?
How old —— is your school bag?
Is Tom German —— brother and sister?
Where's my —— are you?
Is your —— are you from?
Are Tom and Joe —— English book?
Where's —— your classroom?
What's 'tortoise' —— sister in Form 9?
in German?

2 ▶ Word mix
Hier sind einige Wörter durcheinander geraten.
Bringe sie in die richtige Reihenfolge.

Beispiel: **a is very tortoise. clever Trundle**
 Trundle is a very clever tortoise.

1 Debbie my Nick new friends. are and
2 sister. brother are and and Debbie Nick
3 twins are The form. my in
4 new How friends? are your old
5 from? they are Where
6 and sisters. Jenny aren't Sita
7 form. girls The my in two aren't

1 _____
2 _____
3 _____
4 _____
5 _____
6 _____
7 _____

3 ▶ Hiding words (Wörter verstecken)
Verstecke möglichst viele Wörter senkrecht und waagerecht. Die Wörter sollten sich immer kreuzen. Wenn du fertig bist, fülle die Lücken mit x-beliebigen Buchstaben aus. Tausche dein Rätsel mit einem Partner/einer Partnerin und suche die versteckten Wörter. Nimm dazu Farbstifte. Ihr könnt das Spiel auch als Wettspiel machen und eine Suchzeit vereinbaren. Wer die meisten Wörter gefunden hat, hat gewonnen.

Grid contains: WELCOME (with T above O, R, T, T, O, I, S, E going down through O), BOYS, GIRLS crossing TORTOISE vertically.

4 ▶ The fourth word

1 dad	• mum
brother	• _____
2 Frankfurt	• town
Ashton	• _____

3 Germany	• German
England	• _____
4 Oliver	• name
blue	• _____

5 8, 10, 14	• numbers
c, d, f	• _____
6 Jenny	• her book
Ben	• _____ book

New words in combinations 1/2 p.16/A8 - p. 25

auf dem Fußboden	___ ___ _____
Die Zwillinge sind ein **Jahr** alt.	The twins are one _____ old.
Wir **sind nicht** aus der Türkei.	We _____ from Turkey.
ein **schlaues/kluges** Mädchen	a _____ girl
sehr **albern/dumm**	very _____
Natürlich sind sie Zwillinge.	____ _____ they're twins.
einen **Fragebogen** abschreiben	copy a _____
Wer ist dein **Partner**/deine **Partnerin**?	Who's your _____ ?
an/auf der Kingsway High School	___ Kingsway High School
Fragen und **Antworten**	_____ and _____
Schreibt die Wörter auf **Karten**.	Write the words on _____ .
Die **Leute/Menschen** in diesem Dorf sind nett.	The _____ in this village are nice.
Nun,/Also, ist Michael dein Freund?	_____ , is Michael your friend?
eine **tolle/großartige** Lehrerin	a _____ teacher
derselbe Lehrer/**dieselbe** Stadt/**dasselbe** Dorf	____ _____ teacher/town/village
Wer ist dein Deutschlehrer?	_____ ___ your German teacher?
Wie heißt das englische Wort **für** „Schildkröte"?	What's the English word _____ 'Schildkröte'?
unser Lehrer/**unsere** Lehrerin	_____ teacher
fünf **Kinder/Jugendliche** aus demselben Dorf	five _____ from the same village
sein Bruder/**seine** Schwester	____ brother/sister
Tee für mich, bitte.	_____ for me, please.
Ist das die **richtige** Antwort?	Is that the _____ answer?
Was ist hier **falsch**?	What's _____ here?
eine nette **Geschichte** schreiben	write a nice _____
Kannst du meinen Bleistift **sehen**?	Can you _____ my pencil?
Was für eine Farbe hat die **Tür**?	What colour is the _____ ?
Kann ich das **Fenster** öffnen?	Can I open the _____ ?
Deine Schultasche ist im **Schrank**.	Your school bag is in the _____ .
ein Bild am **schwarzen Brett**	a picture on the _____ _____
Wo ist dein **Schulheft**?	Where is your _____ _____ ?
Was kannst du im Klassenzimmer **hören**?	What can you _____ in the classroom?
an die Tafel **schauen**	_____ at the board
Was könnt ihr auf dem **Bild** sehen?	What can you see in the _____ ?
ein **ruhiger** Junge/**ruhiges** Mädchen	a _____ boy/girl
Was kannst du im Klassenzimmer **sagen**?	What can you _____ in the classroom?

Vocab cards

Hier ist ein Vorschlag, wie du mit *Vocab cards* allein oder mit einem Partner/einer Partnerin spielerisch Wörter lernen kannst. Schneide zuerst die Karten aus. Dann mische sie und lege sie in einem Packen mit der Bildseite nach oben. Du legst die erste Karte auf den Tisch und dein Partner/deine Partnerin sagt die englische Bezeichnung. Er/sie dreht die Karte zur Kontrolle um. Hat er/sie Recht, behält er/sie die Karte. Wenn er/sie die Bezeichnung nicht kennt, bist du an der Reihe. Wer zum Schluss die meisten Karten hat, hat gewonnen.

Wenn ihr eure eigenen Karten macht, könnt ihr natürlich auch eine Wendung oder einen ganzen Satz schreiben. Ihr findet dazu genügend Beispiele in den *New words in combinations*. Lest auch den *Tipp „Alles im Kasten"* im Schülerbuch auf Seite 159, wo ihr interessante Anregungen zum Sammeln und Wiederholen findet. Wie euch die Karten auch beim Einprägen neuer Wörter helfen können, erfahrt ihr auf Seite 1.

boy	girl	desk	chair
board	book	page	card
pen	pencil	felt-tip	biro
ruler	rubber	pencil-case	school bag
window	door	floor	cupboard
notice board	box	bin	tortoise

Vocab cards

Wie könnt ihr Bildkarten selbst machen?

Tipp: Überall werden jeden Tag unzählige Zeitungen und Zeitschriften weggeworfen, in denen viele Bilder sind, die sich gut für eigene Bildkarten zum spielerischen Lernen eignen. Wie wäre es, wenn ihr solche Bilder ausschneidet und sammelt? Ihr könnt sie dann auf eine Kopiervorlage kleben, das ganze Blatt mit den Bildern mehrfach kopieren und die Kopien untereinander austauschen. Eine Kopiervorlage findet ihr auf Seite 44.

eight

Vocab cards Hier sind die Bilder noch einmal – nur ist jetzt die Lautschrift auf der Rückseite! Schaut mal nach …

nine

Vocab cards

Eine raffinierte Variante besteht darin, dass auf der Rückseite statt des englischen Wortes nur der Laut steht, auf dem das Wort betont ist, also z.B. für "boy" steht nur ɔɪ. Zum Spiel mit einem Partner/einer Partnerin werden alle Karten mit der Lautschrift nach oben auf den Tisch gelegt und – wie bei Memory – ordentlich verteilt. Wer beginnt, versucht mit Hilfe der Lautschrift das englische Wort zu erraten. Die Karte wird aufgedeckt. Hat er/sie richtig geraten, darf er/sie die Karte behalten und weiterraten, bis er/sie einen Fehler macht. Dann wird die Karte zurückgelegt und der Partner/die Partnerin kommt an die Reihe. Klar, welches Wort er/sie wahrscheinlich erraten wird. Oder? Dieses Spiel schult ungeheuer das Gedächtnis und die Konzentration und macht eine Menge Spaß. Probier es mal aus.

eə	e	ɜː	ɔɪ
ɑː	eɪ	ʊ	ɔː
aɪ	ə	ə	ə
uː	ə	ʌ	uː
ʌ	ɔː	ɔː	ɪ
ɔː	ɪ	ɒ	əʊ

2 My family and my pets

New words in combinations 2/1 p. 26 - p. 28/A1

eine **Familie** aus Chester	a _____ from Chester
ein nettes **Haustier** für Jungen und Mädchen	a nice _____ for boys and girls
Ich bin **bei** einem Freund in Hamburg.	I'm _____ a friend in Hamburg.
meine **Oma** und mein **Opa**	my _____ and my _____
Das ist meine Schwester mit unserer **Katze**.	This is my sister with our ____ .
Ist dein **Hund** ein Männchen?	Is your _____ a 'he'?
Tante Helen und **Onkel** Tom	_____ Helen and _____ Tom
glückliche Haustiere	_____ pets
Das **Kaninchen** ist im Garten.	The _____ is in the garden.
eine **kleine** Stadt in England	a _____ town in England
ein Bild von einem netten **Hamster**	a picture of a nice _____
ein Foto von einem blauen **Wellensittich**	a photo of a blue _____
Mein **Goldfisch** heißt Goldie.	The name of my _____ is Goldie.
Frau und **Herr** Baker	_____ and _____ Baker
Frau Snow ist **Krankenschwester**.	Mrs Snow is a _____ .
Ist Miss Hunt Lehrerin? – Ja, **das stimmt**.	Is Miss Hunt a teacher? – Yes, _____ .
Tee, Ben? Und ein **Keks**?	Tea, Ben? And a _____ ?

1 ▶ Find the right way (Suche den richtigen Weg)

Look. The budgie isn't — her Grandma in Halle.
I can't see the rabbit. It — are in the garden.
A hamster is a nice — in its cage. Where is it?
Here's a photo of my — are you?
Is your dog — sister with her cat.
Jenny is with — isn't in the garden.
How old is — nurse.
The name of the happy — pet for kids.
Debbie and Nick — a 'he' or a 'she'?
Is Ben home — little rabbit is Sue.
I'm Paul. And who — from school?
My uncle is a — your dog?

2 ▶ Where's my pullover?

1 E X E R C I S E
2
3
4
5
6
7
8

1 Copy the words into your … book.
2 Can you … from one to fifty in English?
3 Copy the questionnaire and … it, please.
4 Write the … 'sixty' on the board.
5 The two girls go to the same … .
6 Look at the pictures on … 26 of your book.
7 Trundle is a … .
8 Sita is an … name.

Your pullover is in the … .

eleven

New words in combinations 2/2

p. 28/A2 - p. 31/A13

Debbie, Nick und **ihre** Freunde	Debbie, Nick and _____ friends
Ist der Hund im **Garten**?	Is the dog in the _____ ?
Der Wellensittich ist nicht in **seinem** Käfig.	The budgie isn't in ___ cage.
ein neuer **Käfig**	a new _____
Ich habe/besitze einen tollen Computer.	_____ _____ a great computer.
nichts Neues	_____ new
Fußball**meister/in**	football _____
Er hat/besitzt zwei Hunde.	_____ ____ two dogs.
Was ist in dem **Korb**?	What's in the _____ ?
Der Tee ist in der **Küche**.	The tea is in _____ .
sehr **arm**	very _____
Sie **hat keinen** Bruder.	She _____ _____ a brother.
alt **oder** neu	old ____ new
Wir **haben keine Zeit**.	We _____ ____ _____ .
Meine **Mutter** ist im Garten und …	My _____ is in the garden and …
… mein **Vater** ist in der Küche.	… my _____ is in the kitchen.
Mein Onkel hat ein **Restaurant**.	My uncle has got a _____ .
im Restaurant	____ the restaurant
Was ist los? – Ich habe ein **Problem**.	_____ _____ _____ – I've got a _____ .
Alle meine Freunde sind in derselben Klasse.	_____ my friends are in the same form.
Was ist mit deiner Schwester?	_____ _____ your sister?
Hast du einen Computer? – **Nein**.	Have you got a computer? – ____ , _____ .
Du hast Recht. Entschuldigung.	_____ _____ . _____ .
seine (feste) **Freundin**, ihr (fester) **Freund**	his _____ , her _____
Seine **Eltern** sind tot.	His _____ are dead.
zusammen zur Schule gehen	go to school _____
Jennys Eltern sind **geschieden**.	Jenny's parents are _____ .
seine **Frau/Ehefrau**, ihr **Mann/Ehemann**	his _____ , her _____
Das ist unser neues **Haus**.	This is our new _____ .
auf dem **Baum**	in the _____
Hast du einen Schreibtisch in deinem **Zimmer**?	Have you got a desk in your _____ ?
Nein, ihr Großvater ist nicht **tot**.	No, her grandpa isn't _____ .
Das ist meine **Cousine** Mary.	This is my _____ Mary.
Wir haben zwei **Söhne**.	We've got two _____ .
Ist deine Tante **verheiratet**?	Is your aunt _____ ?
Sie hat eine **Tochter**.	She has got a _____ .

twelve

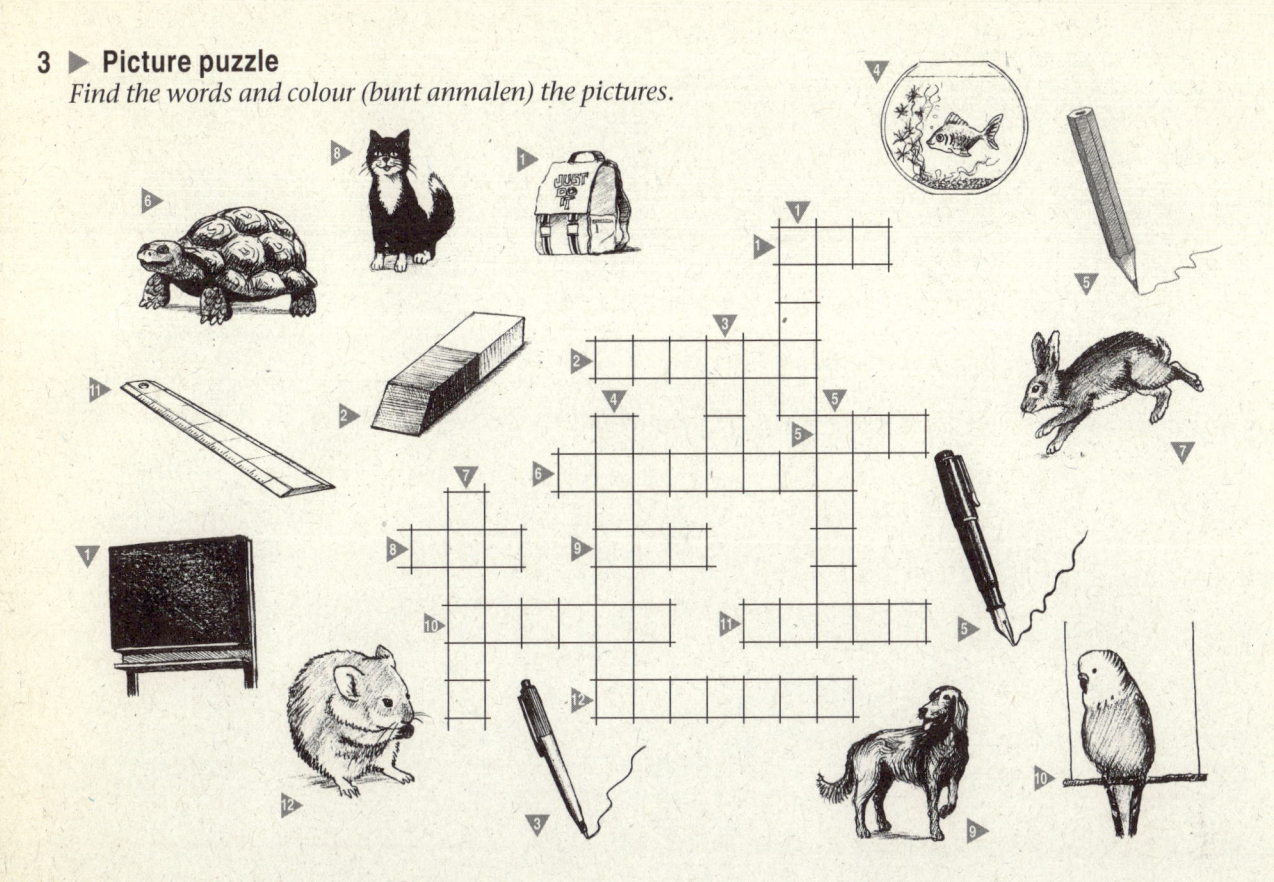

3 ▶ Picture puzzle
Find the words and colour (bunt anmalen) the pictures.

4 ▶ Words, words, words – activity

a *Du hast bis jetzt schon eine ganze Menge englischer Wörter gelernt. Wie gut kannst du sie?
Versuch einmal die deutschen Wörter in dem linken Kasten zu übersetzen. Der rechte Kasten mit den englischen Entsprechungen kann dir dabei helfen.
Tipp: Nimm verschiedenfarbige Marker und kennzeichne in den beiden Kästen die leichten Wörter gelb, die etwas schwierigeren grün und die ganz schweren blau. Schreibe 10 „blaue" Wörter auf und vergleiche deine Liste mit der eines Partners/einer Partnerin.*

German
<u>albern</u> • alle • **<u>Alphabet</u>** • antworten • arm • Baum • Bild • bitte • blau • Bleistift • Bruder • Buch • Buchstabe • Champion • Cousin • Dorf • Ehefrau • Ehemann • einsam • Eltern • Entschuldigung • falsch • Familie • Farbe • Fenster • Frage • Fragebogen • Fußboden • gelb • Geschichte • geschieden • glücklich • Goldfisch • Großstadt • grün • gut • Hamster • Haus • Haustier • heute • hier • hören • Hund • Jahr • Käfig • Kaninchen • Karte (Karteikarte) • Kasten • Katze • Kind • Klassenzimmer • klein • Korb • Krankenschwester • Küche • Kugelschreiber • langweilig • Lehrer/in • Leute • Lied • Lineal • (Hausaufgaben) machen • (Tisch usw.) machen • Mädchen • mit • Morgen • Mutter • Nachmittag • nahe • nett • neu • nichts • öffnen • oft • Onkel • Papierkorb • Partner • Problem • Radiergummi • Restaurant • richtig • rot • ruhig • Satz • schauen • Schildkröte • schlau • Schreibtisch • schwarz • Schwester • sehen • Seite (im Buch) • Stadt • Stuhl • Tätigkeit • Tafel • Tante • Tee • toll • tot • unter • Vater • verheiratet • weiß • Wellensittich • wirklich (nett) • witzig • Zahl • Zimmer • zusammen • Zwillinge

English
activity • afternoon • all • **<u>alphabet</u>** • answer • aunt • basket • bin • biro • black • blue • board • book • boring • box • brother • budgie • cage • card • cat • chair • champion • city • classroom • clever • colour • cousin • cupboard • dead • desk • divorced • do • dog • door • family • father • fine • floor • funny • girl • goldfish • good • great • green • hamster • happy • hear • here • house • husband • kid • kitchen • letter • little • lonely • look • make • married • morning • mother • near • new • nice • nothing • number • nurse • often • open • page • parents • partner • pencil • people • pet • picture • please • poor • problem • question • questionnaire • quiet • rabbit • really • red • restaurant • right • room • rubber • ruler • see • sentence • <u>silly</u> • sister • song • sorry • story • tea • teacher • today • together • tortoise • town • tree • twins • uncle • under • village • white • wife • window • with • wrong • year • yellow

b ***One-minute game***: *Ziel der Übung ist möglichst viele Wörter innerhalb einer Minute mit guter Aussprache zu übersetzen. Also:* silly, all, alphabet … . *Nach einer Minute macht ein Partner/eine Partnerin mit dem nächsten Wort weiter.*

thirteen

New words in combinations 2/3   p. 33/P 7 - p. 39/4

Ich weiß (es) nicht.	_ _____ _____ .
ein **einsamer** Junge	a _____ boy
Jane hat **viele** Freunde.	Jane has got __ ____ ____ friends.
Er hat keinen Freund, **deshalb** ist er einsam.	He hasn't got a friend, _____ he's lonely.
Bens Eltern sind **oft** weg.	Ben's parents are _____ _____ .
Ich habe **heute** keine Zeit.	I haven't got time _____ .
wirklich sehr gut	really _____
ein **langweiliger** Lehrer	a _____ teacher
Wer ist **da**?	Who's _____ ?
am **Nachmittag**	in the _____
Mach dir Notizen, Ben.	_____ _____ , Ben.
Ich denke, Computers sind nicht langweilig.	__ _____ computers aren't boring.
Fragen **beantworten**	_____ questions
fünf **Sätze** bilden	make five _____
Es tut mir leid, daß ich zu **spät** bin.	Sorry I'm _____ .
Lies es **noch einmal**.	Read it _____ .
Hast du unsere **Telefonnummer**?	Have you got our _____ _____ ?

5 ▶ Fast reading game (Lesen um die Wette)
Ersetze den Buchstaben x durch a, e, i, o oder u, um richtige englische Wörter zu bilden, und lies die Wendungen.
Du kannst diese Übung auch als Spiel mit einem Partner/einer Partnerin machen. Wer alle Wendungen am schnellsten lesen kann, gewinnt.

answer	xll thx quxstxxns
answer	thx phxnx
make	a cxgx fxr thx hxmstxr
make	sxntxncxs
wash	thx dxrty pxllxvxr xgxxn
look at	thx pxctxrxs xn pxgx 25
look at	thx nxtxcx bxxrd
write	wxrds xnd nxmbxrs
read	a fxnny stxry xbxxt a gxrl xnd hxr lxttlx whxtx rxbbxt
read	thx sxntxncx xgxxn
swap	a rxlxr fxr a rxbbxr
swap	a pxllxvxr fxr a T-shxrt
go	hxmx txgxthxr
go	tx thx nxw rxstxxrxnt

6 ▶ Positive or negative?
Put the words in the box into two groups. Some (einige) words can be positive or negative.

> **boring** • **clever** • cool • dead
> divorced • fine • funny • good
> happy • late • lonely • lucky
> married • new • nice • old • poor
> quiet • right • silly • wrong

Positive	Negative
clever	boring
_____	_____
_____	_____
_____	_____
_____	_____
_____	_____
_____	_____
_____	_____
_____	_____

3 Around the house

▶ New words in combinations 3/1
p. 40 - p. 42/A2

ein Haus mit einer **Garage**	a house with a _____
ein Haus in einer **kleinen** Stadt	a house in a _____ town
ein **großes** Haus – ein kleines **Auto**	a ____ – a small _____
eine schöne **Wohnung** finden	find a nice _____
eine Wohnung **über** einem Restaurant	a flat _____ a restaurant
ins **Wohnzimmer** gehen	go into the _____-_____
das **Badezimmer** benutzen	use the _____
das **Schlafzimmer** aufräumen	tidy up the _____
um 10 Uhr zu/ins **Bett** gehen	go to _____ at ten
ein Buch auf dem **Bücherregal**	a book on the _____
ein altes **Radio** – ein neuer **Fernseher**	an old _____ – a new _____
um acht zur Schule gehen	go to school ____ eight
aus dem Bad **kommen**	_____ out of the bathroom
Wer kann **mir** helfen?	Who can _____ ____?
Kannst du **mich** hören?	Can you hear _____?
eine **ordentliche/aufgeräumte** Küche	a _____ kitchen
Komm bitte **her**.	_____ _____, please.
die Wohnung **aufräumen**	_____ ____ the flat
die Tafel **sauber machen/wischen**	_____ the board
ein **sauberes** Badezimmer	a _____ bathroom
Es gibt ein Zimmer **oben** und **unten**.	There's a room _____ and _____.

1 ▶ Black and white
Find the opposites.

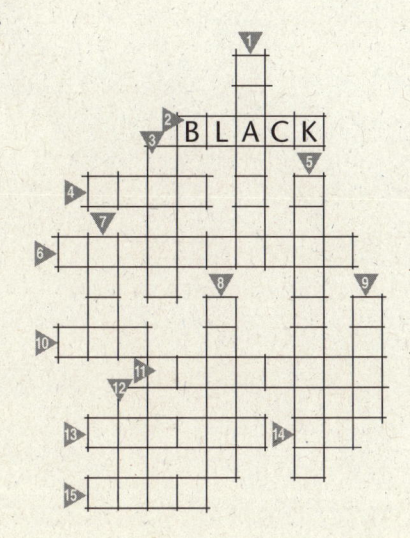

Across ➡
- 2 white
- 4 there
- 6 upstairs
- 10 Mr
- 11 answer
- 13 brother
- 14 yes
- 15 see

Down ⬇
- 1 grandpa
- 3 right
- 5 boyfriend
- 7 under
- 8 silly
- 9 uncle
- 12 husband

fifteen

▶ New words in combinations 3/2
p. 42 - p. 45/A11

Bücher in die Bücherregale **stellen**	_____ books on the bookshelves
Bitte Ruhe. **Setzt euch.**	Quiet please. ____ _____ .
auf dem Boden **sitzen**	_____ on the floor
Tu das nicht noch einmal.	_____ ____ _____ again.
die Mädchen in die Schule **bringen**	_____ the girls to school
Komm bitte **ins** Haus.	Come _____ the house, please.
Dein weißes T-Shirt ist **schmutzig**.	Your white T-shirt is _____ .
Geh nach oben. Aber **renn** nicht.	Go upstairs. But don't _____ .
zu/auf eine Party gehen	go ____ a party
Bina **hat** einen roten Pullover **an**.	Bina is _____ a red pullover.
eine Schildkröte **zeichnen**, einen Comic **lesen**	_____ a tortoise, _____ a comic
mit Freunden in einer Band **spielen**	_____ with friends in a band
zusammen im Garten **arbeiten**	_____ together in the garden
schmutzige Jeans **waschen**	_____ dirty jeans
Komm um fünf **Uhr**.	Come at five _____ .
Sandra **packt** ihre Tasche.	Sandra ___ _____ her bag.
Lasst uns am **Wochenende** Fußball spielen.	Let's play football at the _____ .
einen **Brief an** einen Freund schreiben	write a _____ ____ a friend
auf den Lehrer **warten**	_____ the teacher
Ist Pam **zu Hause/daheim**?	Is Pam ___ _____ ?
Lasst uns das **Abendessen zubereiten**.	Let's _____ _____ .
im Wohnzimmer **fernsehen**	_____ ____ in the living-room
ein Video/einen Film **ansehen**	_____ a video/a film
Guck/Schau (mal) – da ist Sita.	_____ – there's Sita.
das **Geschirr abwaschen**	_____ the _____
Warum rennst du?	_____ are you running?
Sei leise. Jane **schläft**.	Be quiet. Jane is _____ .
Schönes Wochenende.	_____ __ _____ _____ .

2 ▶ Word mix

- I think washing the dishes. Jenny is   I think Jenny _____
- kids The packing the for weekend. are   _____
- his homework Ben room. in doing is English his   _____
- this you exercise, please? help Ben Can with   _____
- help you, got Sorry, haven't I time. can't   _____

New words in combinations 3/3

p. 46/P1 - p. 51

eine neue Cassette **hören**	_____ ____ a new cassette
ein Wort **an** die Tafel schreiben	write a word _____ the board
Wie bitte? Ich kann dich nicht hören.	_____ ? I can't hear you.
ein **Traumhaus** zeichnen	draw a _____ _____
Was für einen **Tag** haben wir heute? – **Samstag**.	What _____ is today? – It's_____ .
mit einem Freund/einer Freundin **reden**	_____ ___ a friend
ein Baumhaus **bauen**	_____ a tree house
Bring die Kiste **hinauf** in dein Zimmer.	Take the box ____ to your room.
herunterkommen	come _____
ein **Stück** Papier/Holz/Kuchen	a _____ ____ paper/wood/cake
eine weitere Frage	_____ _____ question
Sie hat nur ein **Kind**.	She's only got one _____ .
ein Film/eine Geschichte für **Kinder**	a film/a story for _____
auf einer **Mauer** sitzen	sit on a _____
zu klein/groß/alt	_____ small/big/old
Sei vorsichtig.	___ _____ .
wegfliegen	_____ away
London ist eine große **Stadt**.	London is a big _____ .
Sie kann **sich** nicht **bewegen**.	She can't _____ .
Ich habe **nur/bloß** einen Bleistift	I've _____ got a pencil.

3 ▶ What can you do?
Find the right verbs (Verben) and add (hinzufügen) the words in the box.

		G	O	away/to school/home/to bed/ *to the toilet*
	L	I		to a new cassette/to a CD/to your parents/
		W	A	a video/a film/tennis/
		W	R	a story/to a friend/a sentence on the board/
		S	I	down/in a tree/on a wall/
		U	S	a pencil/a ruler/the bathroom/
		W	A	here/at the supermarket/
		P	L	football/with friends/
		R	E	a text/a story/the words on the board/
		W	O	together/with a partner/at a restaurant/
		D	R	a picture/a tree/a dog/a car/

Word box: a game / a dream house / a letter / a rubber / in bed / TV / in the car / on a chair / **to the toilet** / to the radio / in the kitchen

▶ New words in combinations 3/4

p.52/1 - p. 53/5

Was für ein **Datum** haben wir heute?	What _____ is it today?
ein **Wand**kalender	a wall _____
in diesem/im nächsten **Monat**	this/next _____
Ich habe diese/in dieser **Woche** keine Zeit.	I haven't got time this _____ .
am 8. **Juni**	____ 8th _____
Gehen wir doch zum Film am **Dienstag**.	Let's go to the film ____ _____ .
morgen früh/Abend	_____ morning/evening
am nächsten/nächstes Wochenende	_____ week
Wann hast du **Geburtstag**?	When's your _____ ?
Wie spät ist es?	_____ ____ ___ ___ ?
um **Viertel nach** fünf/5.15/17.15	at _____ _____ five
um **halb** sechs/5.30/17.30	at _____ _____ five
um **Viertel vor** sechs/5.45/17.45	at _____ ____ six
Wann kannst du hier sein?	_____ can you be here?
von 10.00 **bis** 12.00 warten	wait from ten ____ twelve
am Abend fernsehen	watch TV ___ _____ _____
Tag und **Nacht** arbeiten	work day and _____

4 ▶ At, in, on, to?
'an/am' in German:
Fill in the missing words **at, in, on, to**.

1 wait *at* the door

2 go _____ the door

3 come _____ the board

4 Open your books _____ page 20.

5 Write the answer _____ the board, please.

6 Can you come _____ the weekend.

7 Is your party _____ Saturday or Sunday?

8 Do your homework _____ your room.

9 You can put the poster _____ the wall.

10 His birthday is _____ 14th July.

11 The film is _____ three o'clock.

12 I'm writing a letter _____ a friend.

13 Write your name _____ the door.

14 Mrs Miller is a teacher _____ our school.

5 ▶ Odd word out

1 red, yellow, biro, green
2 you, my, they, she
3 hall, poster, bed, bookshelf
4 rabbit, hamster, pet, budgie
5 desk, chair, sofa, house
6 three, fifth, first, tenth
7 lonely, funny, red, nice
8 pen, swap, book, computer

1 *biro* _____   5 _____

2 _____   6 _____

3 _____   7 _____

4 _____   8 _____

▶ Now you
Write two Odd words out and ask your partner.

1 _____

2 _____

4 Happy birthday!

▶ **New words in combinations 4/1**   p. 54 - p. 56/A3

von einem neuen Computer **träumen**	_____ _____ a new computer
einen schönen **Traum** haben	have a nice _____
ein Buch **über** London lesen	read a book _____ London
eine Geburtstags**kuchen** mit elf **Kerzen**	a birthday _____ with eleven _____
Orangensaft für Sita und mich	_____ _____ for Sita and me
ein nettes **Geschenk** für Richard	a nice _____ for Richard
Keine **Pommes frites** für mich.	No _____ for me.
Eis essen	eat _____
viele Freunde haben	have _____ _____ friends
eine Party **feiern**	_____ a party
ein sehr guter **Einfall**	a very good _____
Du kannst ein Video **bekommen**.	You can _____ a video.
die Zeit und das Datum einer **Einladung**	the time and the date of an _____
Müssen wir ein Bild malen?	_____ we draw a picture?
deiner Klasse über einen Ausflug **berichten**	_____ your form about a trip
Mach dein Bett, **dann** kannst du spielen.	Make your bed, _____ you can play.
Wir **müssen** die Übung **nicht** machen.	We _____ do the exercise.
Wir **dürfen nicht** zu spät sein.	We _____ be late.
Fußball spielen und dann ein Lied **singen**	play _____ and then _____ a song
mit dem Rad zur Schule **fahren**	_____ __ _____ to school

1 ▶ Missing letters
Fill in the missing letters to make combinations.

1. open and read a
2. go into and tidy up a
3. draw and look at a
4. sit and read under a
5. read and tell a
6. go into and work in the
7. play and watch a
8. open and clean a
9. make and watch a
10. write and spell your
11. wait for and talk to
12. sing and listen to a

#						
1	L	E	T			
2		O	O			
3			C	T		
4		R				
5			O			
6	G		D			
7	G		E			
8		N	D			
9			E	O		
10	N		E			
11	E	O				
12	O					

nineteen

▶ **New words in combinations 4/2**　　　　　　　　　　　　　　　　　　p.57/A4 - p. 58/A7

ein nettes Geschenk **suchen**	_____ ____ a nice present
eine **Schachtel Pralinen** öffnen	open a _____ ___ _____
eine **Armbanduhr** tragen	wear a _____
ein **teures** neues Auto	an _____ new car
ein **billiges** Bücherregal suchen	look for a _____ bookshelf
einen **Schal** tragen	wear a _____
Wie wär's mit einem Eis?	_____ _____ an ice-cream?
Noch hier?	_____ here?
von weißen **Mäusen** träumen	dream about white _____
auf einem Stuhl **stehen**	_____ on a chair
sich unter einen Baum **stellen**	go and _____ under a tree
vor dem Haus warten	wait ___ _____ ___ the house
hinter dem Auto halten	stop _____ the car
mit einem **Mann** auf der Straße sprechen	talk to a _____ in the street
eine geschiedene **Frau** mit drei Kindern	a divorced _____ with three children
um fünf Uhr **zurück**kommen	come _____ at five o'clock
sich auf eine **Bank** setzen	sit down on a _____
eine Garage **neben** unserem Haus	a garage _____ ___ our house
ein Garten **zwischen** zwei Häusern	a garden _____ two houses

2 ▶ Word mix
Put the words in the right order and make sentences.

Put here, please. **orange juice** the　　　_____

come back Can three o'clock? you at　　_____

for I'm a looking mum. birthday **present** for my　_____

birthday present. **bike** new great is a A　_____

bookshelf. for I'm a looking **cheap**　　　_____

nice weekend He's **dreaming** in a about Ashton.　_____

looking for book a Mrs Keller Chester. is about　_____

children. three **divorced woman** with small a She's　_____

under the tree. Let's **bench** on this sit　_____

to The garage the is **next** restaurant.　_____

two big is Our houses. **between** garden　_____

please? What now, **time** is it　　　　　_____

3 ▶ Let's talk about people
Find words and write them down in two groups. How many words can you find?

```
N M A R R I E D H P N R G G Y Q L
B R I T I S H X N O I I R K T U U
G B I G X W I F E O C P A F G I C
B H U S B A N D A R E A N A R E K
O Y P P D I N D I A N R D T A T Y
Y G I R L F R I E N D E P H N M T
F C G D H A P P Y C H N A E D A W
R L E I F R T G I R L T M R M N O
I E R V A S E A B O Y S P T A F M
E V M O M I A R C O U S I N D U A
N E A R I S C P A R T N E R O N N
D R N C L T H T M O T H E R L N T
A C I E Y E E H W S I L L Y D Y W
U N L D E R R C J L I T T L E E I
N B R O T H E R I B O R I N G D N
T D E A D U N C L E F S M A L L S
```

▶ **Group 1: People**

husband, _____

_____

_____

_____

_____

▶ **Group 2: How can people be?**

happy, _____

_____

_____

_____

_____

Now make combinations and sentences.

1 *a happy man, my little brother,* _____

_____

_____

_____

_____

_____

_____

_____

2 *Her husband is British. My cousin is very clever.* _____

_____

_____

_____

_____

_____

_____

twenty-one

▶ **New words in combinations 4/3**   p. 59/A8 - p. 63/P 8

einen Dialog **spielen**	_____ a dialogue
zusammen singen und **tanzen**	sing and _____ together
auf eine Mauer **klettern**	_____ a wall
Warum? – **Weil** ich nach Hause gehen muss.	Why? – _____ I must go home.
im Bus neue Wörter lernen	learn new words ___ ___ ___
eine Menge **belegte Brote** machen	make lots of _____
am **Tisch** sitzen	sit at the _____
nur einen Schal haben	have got _____ one scarf
erst drei Jahre alt	_____ three years old
Unser Geburtstagsgeschenk. **Bitte sehr.**	Our birthday present. _____ _____.
Los, komm! Es ist spät.	_____ _____. It's late.
ein Bild **von** deiner Schule zeichnen	draw a picture ___ your school
Bitte **lache** nicht **über** ihn.	Please don't _____ ___ him.
eine Namens**liste** anfertigen	make a _____ of names
deine/n Lehrer/in **fragen**	_____ your teacher
eine Menge **Hausaufgaben** haben	have lots of _____

4 ▶ **Read, say and write**

Across ➡
- 4 əˈgen
- 5 ˈwɪmɪn
- 6 ˈkʌzn
- 8 ˈkʌbəd
- 12 ˌdaʊnˈsteəz
- 13 kɑː
- 14 klaɪm
- 15 ˈkælɪndə
- 16 lɑːf
- 17 ˈbentʃɪz

Down ⬇
- 1 dɑːns
- 2 ˈrestrɒnt
- 3 ˌʌpˈsteəz
- 7 ˈsænwɪdʒ
- 9 skɑːvz
- 10 ˈkændl
- 11 ˈpɪktʃə

Just for fun

Tom Your cat is saying 'bow-wow'!
Sue Well, yes. She is a clever cat.
         She can speak other languages.

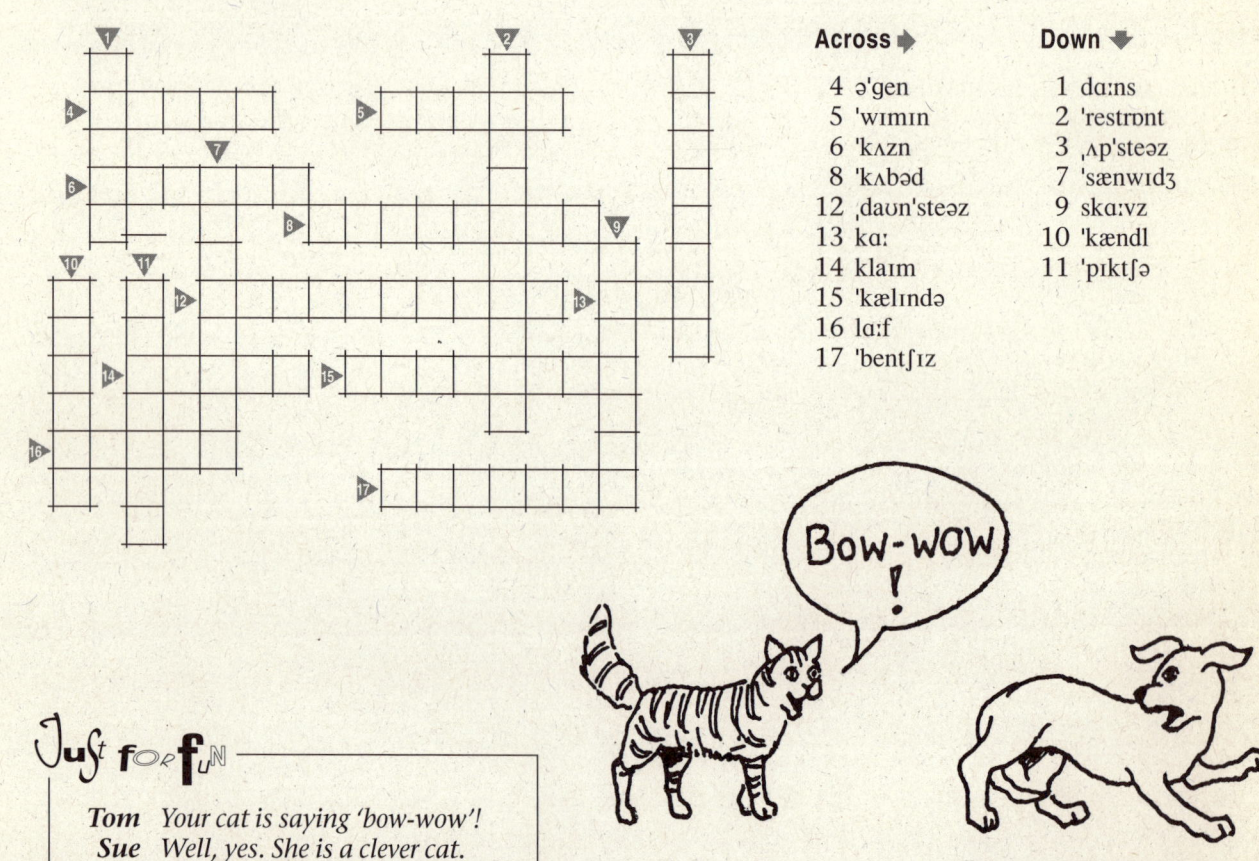

▶ **New words in combinations 4/4**   p. 66 - p. 69/4

die Kiste **hinstellen**	_____ _____ the box
Brote **essen** und ...	_____ sandwiches and ...
Saft **trinken**	_____ juice
allein und einsam	be _____ and lonely
Können wir ihm ein Geschenk **geben**?	Can we _____ him a present?
zum **Supermarkt** gehen	go to the _____
jetzt **in Schwierigkeiten** sein	be ____ _____ now
auf **die anderen** Kinder warten	wait for _____ _____ children
eine Menge **Geld** geben	give lots of _____
Fünf **Pfund** ist sehr teuer.	Five _____ is very expensive.
Was **kostet** das Eis?	_____ _____ ____ the ice-cream?
Was **kosten** die Pralinen?	_____ _____ _____ the chocolates?
Das Spiel **kostet** £5.	The game ____ £5.
Kuchen im Supermarkt **kaufen**	_____ cake at the supermarket
Sie **wünschen**?	_____ __ _____ _____ ?
Kann/Darf ich jetzt gehen?	_____ / _____ I go now?
einen **Verkäufer**/eine **Verkäuferin** suchen	look for an _____
mit einem **Kunden**/einer **Kundin** sprechen	talk to a _____
Ich sehe mich nur um.	____ _____ _____ .

5 ▶ **This and that**
Make combinations with words from the box.

> children • down • drink • go • mother • night • no • old • play •
> sisters • then • there • tomorrow • **white** • wives • women

1 black and *white* _____
2 new and _____
3 here and _____
4 up and _____
5 now and _____
6 yes and _____
7 come and _____
8 work and _____

9 eat and _____
10 day and _____
11 today and _____
12 men and _____
13 husbands and _____
14 father and _____
15 brothers and _____
16 parents and _____

twenty-three

5 Kingsway High School

▶ New words in combinations 5/1

p.70 - p. 72/A4

Schul**uniformen** tragen	wear school _____
weiße/**graue** Mäuse	white/ _____ mice
ein **Schüler**/eine **Schülerin** in meiner Klasse	a _____ in my form
Mittagessen in der **Schulmensa**	_____ in the school _____
Was habt ihr nach der **Pause**?	What have you got after the _____ ?
Das Fußballspiel ist um 3.30 Uhr **nachmittags**.	The football game is at 3.30 _____ .
um 9.00 Uhr **vormittags**	at 9.00 _____
Was ist montags die erste **Unterrichtsstunde**?	What's the first _____ on Mondays?
heute keinen **Unterricht** haben	have no _____ today
am Morgen/morgens in die Schule gehen	go to school ___ ___ _____
Sie ist **am Nachmittag/nachmittags** zu Hause.	She's at home ___ ___ _____ .
am Abend/abends Radio hören	listen to the radio ___ ___ _____
in der Nacht/nachts arbeiten	work ___ _____
Die **Schulversammlung** ist von 10.50 bis 11.05.	_____ is from 10.50 to 11.05.
jede Frau, **jeder** Mann, **jedes** Kind	_____ woman, _____ man, _____ child
Debbie ist in einer **Schauspiel**gruppe.	Debbie is in a _____ group.
ein Sport-/Tennis-/Fußball**klub**	a sports/tennis/football _____
Sport treiben	do _____
auf der ersten Seite des **Prospekts**/der **Broschüre**	on the first page of the _____
Information(en) am Schwarzen Brett finden	find _____ on the notice board
von Mittwoch **bis** Samstag	_____ Wednesday ____ Saturday
Um welche Zeit **beginnt** der Unterricht?	What time do lessons _____ ?
einen Satz/einen Brief/ die Arbeit **beenden**	_____ a sentence/a letter/ work
belegte Brote von zu Hause **mitbringen**	_____ sandwiches from home
nach dem Frühstück – **vor** der Schule	_____ breakfast – _____ school
zum **Judo**unterricht gehen	go to _____ class

1 ▶ The fourth word

1	7 o'clock	• breakfast
	12 o'clock	• _____
2	beds	• make
	dishes	• _____

3	open	• close
	start	• _____
4	home	• dining-room
	school	• _____

5	evening	• in the evening
	night	• _____
6	brother	• sister
	husband	• _____

2 ▶ All good things come in threes
(Aller guten Dinge sind drei.)

What three words go together?
Example: 'tired, sleep, dream'

1 tired	a aunt	a bench
2 father	b book	b boyfriend
3 men	c chair	c children
4 uncle	d dialogue	d children
5 friend	e evening	e city
6 sit	f flat	f cousin
7 read	g girlfriend	g dream
8 make	h mother	h month
9 act	i pencil	i night
10 morning	j sleep	j pencil-case
11 village	k tea	k director
12 biro	l town	l room
13 house	m week	m sandwiches
14 day	n women	n sentence
15 word	o word group	o story

1						
j						
g						

3 ▶ A new letter – a new word
Example: like → bike

1 big → *bag* Put your things in the … .
2 think → _____ … you very much.
3 bad → _____ Let's go to … now.
4 sing → _____ Let's sing a … .
5 tall → _____ … your partner about it.
6 fall → _____ … in the questionnaire.
7 make → _____ Let's make a birthday … .
8 date → It's _____ . Let's go.

4 ▶ Comb puzzle (Kammrätsel)

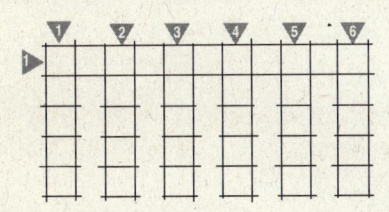

Down ⬇

1 father : mother – boys : …
2 opposite of before
3 opposite of clean
4 Put the words in the right … .
5 car : garage – people : …
6 opposite of wrong

Across ➡

1 your grandfather's wife

5 ▶ Find the right way
Make sentences.

It's not funny,	about your town.
Open your books	is on the notice board.
Let's swap	so don't laugh.
Can you answer	on your test.
Is this	at page 71.
The two	stickers.
More information	on the bench.
Take this box	your pencil-case?
Write your name	at eight in our school.
Put the film	speak English?
Sit down	downstairs.
Make your bed	girls are twins.
What's	all the questions?
Can you	in the video recorder.
Collect information	for dinner today?
Lessons start	after breakfast.

6 ▶ Picture puzzle

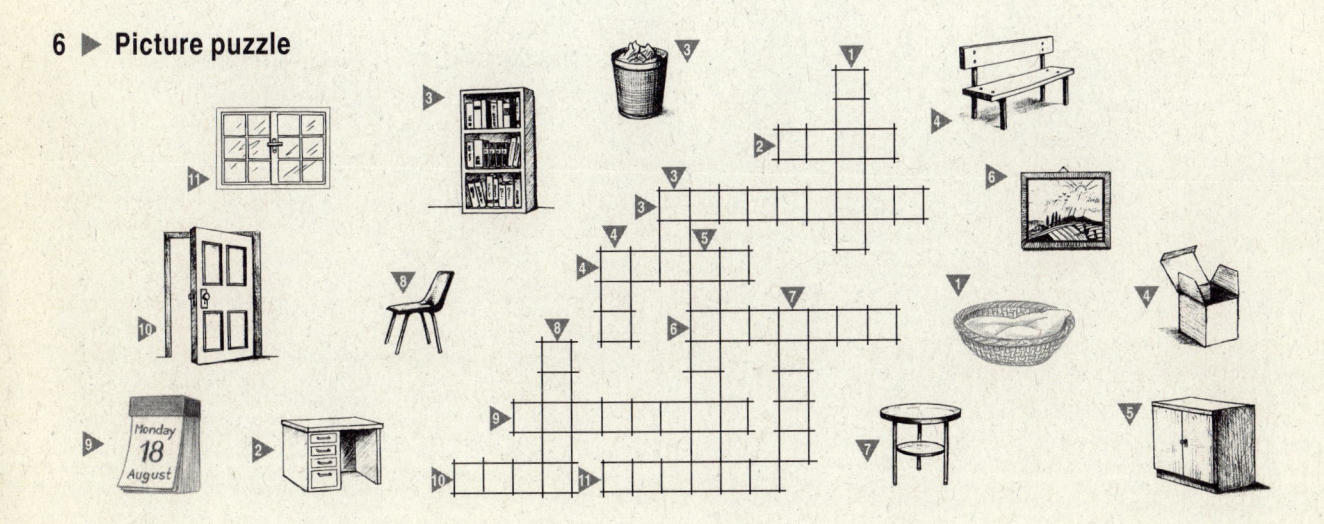

▶ **New words in combinations 5/2**

p.73/A5 - p. 74/A9

Ist das dein neuer **Stundenplan**?	Is this your new _____ _____?
ein **Schulfach** mögen/nicht mögen	like/hate a _____ _____
Wo ist Ben? – Er spielt auf der **Straße**.	Where's Ben? – He's playing in the _____.
Liebe Linda, **lieber** Dave, …	_____ Linda and Dave, …
Versuche viele Wörter zu sammeln	_____ _____ collect lots of words.
sonntags/jeden Sonntag	_____ _____
sonntags morgens/nachmittags	_____ _____ _____ /afternoons
an **Wochenenden** Tennis spielen	play tennis _____ _____
Was für Fächer **magst** du in der Schule?	What subjects do you _____ at school?
Ist Mathematik dein **Lieblings**fach?	Is maths your _____ subject?
ein Pullover in drei **verschiedenen** Farben	a pullover in three _____ colours
Viele liebe Grüße (von) …	_____, …
Briefmarken kaufen/tauschen	buy/swap _____
Plakate von Popstars **sammeln**	_____ posters of pop stars
in einem **Theaterstück** (mit)spielen	act in a _____
Trete unserem **Schach**klub **bei**, Max.	_____ our _____ club, Max.
sich an Wochenenden/in Raum 3 **treffen**	_____ at weekends/in room 3
von Freunden **Fotos machen**	_____ _____ of friends
Englisch in der Schule **lernen**	_____ English at school
sich montags in der **Turnhalle** treffen	meet in the _____ on Mondays
Sie **liebt** das Lied, er **hasst** es.	She _____ the song, he _____ it.

7 ▶ **Missing letters**
Find two missing letters and finish a word. Use the same letters and start a new word.

Example: Mar (__ __) air.
The missing letters are 'ch'.
The two words are 'March' and 'chair'.

1 dr   (__ __) ay
2 cous   (__ __) formation
3 pho   (__ __) xt
4 mon   (__ __) ink
5 wom   (__ __) swer
6 befo   (__ __) ad
7 ti   (__ __) et
8 de   (__ __) ound
9 fini   (__ __) elf
10 lo   (__ __) ry
11 ha   (__ __) am
12 less   (__ __) ly
13 bi   (__ __) om
14 troub (__ __) arn
15 tab   (__ __) tter

8 ▶ **Word mix**
Put the words in the right order and make sentences.

1 Haven't a **timetable**? new you got
2 friends Do **collect stamps**, your too?
3 **subject**? your Is favourite maths
4 Is a there school? at your **notice board**
5 the When's **break**? lunch
6 in you buy canteen? **lunch** school the Can

1 _____
2 _____
3 _____
4 _____
5 _____
6 _____

New words in combinations 5/3
p.75/A11 - p. 84

als **Au-pair**(-Mädchen/-Junge) arbeiten	work as an _____
Sie geht **immer** um 10 Uhr schlafen.	She _____ goes to bed at 10 o'clock.
Er isst **nie** Schokolade.	He _____ eats chocolate.
um 7.30 Uhr **aufstehen**	_____ at 7.30
Was gibts zum **Frühstück**?	What's for _____?
Um diese Zeit ist sie **auf der Arbeit**.	At this time she's ___ _____.
die Kinder **von** der Schule **abholen**	_____ the children _____ school
Ich gehe nicht oft in den **Park**.	I don't often go to the _____.
Was machst du **gewöhnlich** sonntags?	What do you _____ do on Sundays?
Er hilft mir **manchmal**.	He _____ helps me.
ein **freies** Wochenende	a _____ weekend
Auf geht's ins **Kino**.	Let's go to the _____.
Zuerst haben wir Englisch, dann Mathematik.	_____ we've got English, then Maths.
mit dem Fahrrad im Dorf **herum**fahren	ride your bike _____ the village
bei einem **Spiel/Wettkampf** zuschauen	watch a _____
Ich mag den Film nicht. Er ist **so** langweilig.	I don't like the film. It's ____ boring.
Sonntags **schläft** er oft **lange**.	He often _____ _____ on Sundays.
das **heutige** Radioprogramm hören	listen to _____ radio programme
Das heutige Spiel **ist etwas Besonderes**.	Today's match ___ _____.
Was gibts morgen **im Radio**?	What's ____ ____ _____ tomorrow?
Das ist ein sehr **schlechter Pass**.	That's a very _____ _____.
Das ist ein **Tor**. Zwei zu null **für** Liverpool.	That's a _____. Two nil ____ Liverpool
in der **Halbzeitpause** Orangensaft trinken	drink orange juice at _____
eine **Hälfte**, zwei **Hälften**	one _____, two _____
Orangen/Apfelsinen mögen	like _____
Nick, **zieh** deinen dreckigen Pullover **aus**.	Nick, _____ _____ your dirty pullover.
Putz bitte deine **Schuhe**.	Please clean your _____.
ein **schrecklicher/furchtbarer** Junge	a _____ boy

9 ▶ Sound check

1 klʌb → _ _ _ _
2 lʌntʃ → _ _ _ _ _
3 kænˈtiːn → _ _ _ _ _ _ _
4 ˈlesn → _ _ _ _ _
5 spɔːt → _ _ _ _ _
6 əˈsembli → _ _ _ _ _ _ _ _
7 breɪk → _ _ _ _ _

10 ▶ Making new words
Find the right words from the box and make new words with words from the box.
(1) = one word, (2) = two words, (-) = use a hyphen (Bindestrich)

> bed • book • drama • felt • English • foot • football • girl • gold • **home** • living
> lunch • notice • **orange** • **pencil** • school • school • stamp • super • time • week

1 _home_work (1)	2 _orange_ juice (2)	3 _pencil_-case (-)
4 _____ table (1)	5 _____ friend (1)	6 _____ market (1)
7 _____ shelf (1)	8 _____ room (-)	9 _____ ball (1)
10 _____ board (2)	11 _____ fish (1)	12 _____ team (2)
13 _____ tip (-)	14 _____ teacher (2)	15 _____ break (2)
16 _____ room (1)	17 _____ group (2)	18 _____ uniform (2)
19 _____ club (2)	20 _____ subject (2)	21 _____ end (1)

11 ▶ Four-letter words

A	E	1 The text is on the first … of the book.
A	E	2 Where's the budgie? It's not in its … .
A	E	3 What's Peter's …? – Meyer.
A	E	4 Is 8th June the right …?
A	E	5 Let's play a computer … together.
A	E	6 You must run. You're … .
A	E	7 The opposite of 'like'.
A	E	8 The opposite of 'give'.

12 ▶ Race against time (Wettlauf mit der Zeit)
Put the words in the right order and read them as fast as you can (so schnell wie du kannst). Half a minute is super. One minute is not bad. Two minutes is OK.

1 Please at your home. homework do

2 the after your lesson. Tidy up classroom

3 speak Don't lesson. English in the German

4 at Please books 85. your page open

5 the words right Put order. in

6 sentence? I next Can the read

7 please? I window, the Can open

8 'Fehler' is 'English'? in What

13 ▶ Words in a spider's web (Spinnennetz)
Find the right words. They're all four-letter words and end in -e.

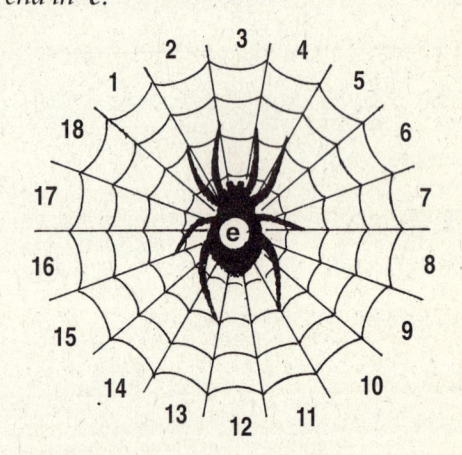

1 What colour is your car? – It's … .
2 I'm sorry. I can't … to your party.
3 Ann's mother only works in the mornings, so she's at … in the afternoons.
4 Tom's grandparents … in a big house in a town near Chester.
5 What … is the English lesson?
6 Come … a minute, please.
7 Let's … a birthday cake together.
8 I usually sleep … at the weekend.
9 Carol's birthday isn't in May, it's in … .
10 Mr Martin always takes off one … at half-time.
11 In the camera club you can … photos and learn about cameras.
12 How are you? – I'm …, thanks.
13 Can you … me your new phone number?
14 My mother is dead. And my father has got a new … . Her name is Karin.
15 Read the second word in the third … .
16 I don't … this video. I think it's boring.
17 I like rabbits and hamsters, but I don't like … .
18 Nick can't … his bike with Ben.

6 Out shopping

New words in combinations 6/1 p.88 - p.90/A2

Einkaufen/Einkäufe	_____
Gehen wir **einkaufen**.	Let's ____ _____ .
eine **Zeitschrift** anschauen/kaufen/lesen	look at/buy/read a _____
Kleidung/Kleider tragen/ausziehen/waschen	wear/take off/wash _____
sich die Bilder in einer **Mode**zeitschrift ansehen	look at the pictures in a _____ magazine
an den **Strand** gehen	go to the _____
Badeanzüge mitbringen	bring _____
Das **hell**gelbe Auto ist neu.	The _____ yellow car is new.
ein Bild **von** Picasso	a picture ____ Picasso
Wo ist meine **Badehose**?	Where are my _____ - _____ ?
Nicks neu **kurze Hose** ist blau.	Nick's new _____ are blue.
rote Schuhe oder **Sandalen**	red shoes or _____
ein sauberes weißes **Hemd** anhaben	wear a clean white _____
ein roter Pullover mit **Schottenmuster**	a red _____ pullover
Komm herein und leg deine **Jacke** ab.	Come in and take off your _____ .
einen kurzen **Rock** mit Schottenmuster tragen	wear a short tartan _____
Magst du mein neues rotes **Kleid**?	Do you like my new red _____ ?
Kannst du mir **zeigen**, wo das Bad ist?	Can you _____ me where the bathroom is?
ein sehr/wirklich **hübsches** Jackett	a really/very _____ jacket
Die **Bluse** sieht gut/hübsch/toll **aus**.	The _____ _____ good/pretty/great.
Ist meine (lange) **Hose** im Schlafzimmer?	Are my _____ in the bedroom?
weiße/schmutzige/saubere **Socken/Strümpfe**	white/dirty/clean _____
Wie teuer sind **diese** Schuhe?	How much are _____ shoes?
Was hältst du von dem **rechten** Pullover?	What about the pullover ____ _____ ?
Ich mag den roten Rock **links**.	I like the red skirt ____ ____ .
Ich glaube, du **brauchst** neue Schuhe.	I think you _____ new shoes.
Ich glaube, der Rock/das Kleid ist zu **lang**.	I think the skirt/the dress is too _____ .
Bitte leg **die** alten Kleider **da** in den Korb.	Please put _____ old clothes in the basket.
Preise fallen oder **steigen**.	_____ go down or ____ ____ .
Vielleicht hast du Recht.	_____ you're right.
Das Kleid ist teuer, aber ich mag es **trotzdem**.	The dress is expensive, but I _____ like it.
Mrs Baker **will** Jeans für Debbie haben.	Mrs Baker _____ jeans for Debbie.
Spaß haben/sich amüsieren auf einer Fete	_____ _____ at a party

twenty-nine

▶ **New words in combinations 6/2**   p. 91/A3 - p. 93/A9

samstags in einen **Judokurs** gehen	go to a judo _____ on Saturdays
einige/ein paar Fragen stellen	ask _____ questions
etwas Geld/Zeit/Schokolade haben	have _____ money/time/chocolate
mit **Spielzeug** spielen	play with _____
Bücher **tragen**	_____ books
Probiere die Schuhe an, bevor du sie kaufst.	_____ the shoes _____ before you buy them.
Diese Bluse **steht** dir **gut**.	This blouse _____ _____ on you.
Sei doch nicht so **dumm/dämlich**.	Don't be so _____.
Er ist **wie** sein Vater.	He's _____ his father.
einen Pullover **verkehrt herum** anhaben	wear a pullover ____ _____ _____ _____
Welch ein **schöner**, neuer **Hut**.	What a _____ new _____.
Kannst du mich am Freitag **anrufen**?	Can you _____ me on Friday?
Was ist denn das **Ding** auf dem Tisch?	What's that _____ on the table?
Essen/Lebensmittel im Supermarkt kaufen	buy _____ at the supermarket
zu viel für einen alten Computer **bezahlen**	_____ too much for an old computer

1 ▶ Plurals
Fill in the missing plurals of the nouns.

one **box**	Put down the two _____.
one **price**	The _____ are different.
one **wife**	You can't have two _____.
one **half**	There's a break between the _____ _____.
one **mouse**	She's got two white _____.
one **shelf**	Two new _____? – OK.
one **bench**	There are lots of _____.
one **match**	go to two football _____
one **man**	Do you know the two _____?
one **child**	The two _____ are twins.
one **city**	two big English _____
one **watch**	two expensive _____
one **hobby**	They've got the same _____.
one **woman**	The two _____ are nurses.

2 ▶ One word – ten things
What is 'it'? Find out from the box.

> a drama class • a special shop • fashion •
> his bed • your name • that toy •
> the letter • the radio • your bike •
> your homework

1 He only listens to **it** in the car.
2 She sometimes goes to **it** for women's clothes.
3 Do you ride **it** to school?
4 I think he's too old and he doesn't want to play with **it**.
5 Can you spell **it** for me, please?
6 Why do you think **it**'s boring?
7 She goes to **it** in the afternoons.
8 Read **it** again and tell me what you think of it.
9 Please do **it** at home.
10 He makes **it** before breakfast.

the radio _____

_____

_____

_____

_____

_____

_____

_____

_____

thirty

3 ▶ Odd word out
- father grandfather husband man uncle
- book magazine questionnaire brochure
- calendar day week month night year
- silly lonely happy dirty only

_____

_____

4 ▶ Words looking for friends

> a job • a letter • a sentence • a song •
> a story • a tree • a video •
> a window • a word • bed • clothes •
> English • **information** • stamps •
> a swimming-pool • toys • lunch •
> your room

need and ask for	*information*
try on and wear	_____
play with and look for	_____
say and spell	_____
sing and listen to	_____
write and finish	_____
go to and be in	_____
make and eat	_____
buy and collect	_____
make and watch	_____
learn and speak	_____
open and clean	_____
sit in and watch TV in	_____
look for and get	_____
go to and swim in	_____
climb and sit in	_____
copy and complete	_____
read and tell	_____

5 ▶ Opposites and similar words
Put the opposites and similar (bedeutungsähnlich) words in the right boxes.

> **after** • behind • big • **clever** •
> dirty • downstairs • expensive •
> good • hate • kids • little • love •
> never • no • old • pretty • right •
> right • short • slow • **stupid** •
> super • terrible • usually

	similar word	opposite
before		*after*
silly	*stupid*	*clever*
like		
children		
long		
wrong		
left		
in front of		
yes		
always		
small		
nice		
great		
clean		
upstairs		
quick		
bad		
new		
cheap		

▶ **New words in combinations 6/3**   p. 93/A10 - p.101

in einem **Kaufhaus** einkaufen gehen	go shopping at a _____ _____
Stelle **alles** auf den Boden.	Put _____ on the floor.
Kennst du meine Telefonnummer?	Do you _____ my phone number?
Ein **Punkt** für jede richtige Antwort.	One _____ for every right answer.
Kannst du dich an ihren Namen **erinnern**?	Can you _____ her name?
Mach dir keine **Sorgen um** mich.	Don't _____ _____ me.
Ist das deine **Größe**?	Is that your _____ ?
Entschuldigung./Entschuldigen Sie.	_____ _____ .
Du kannst hier nicht **anhalten/stoppen**.	You can't _____ here.
Was ist los?/Was geht hier vor?	_____ _____ ?
Es **passiert/geschieht** oft nachts.	It often _____ at night.
Es ist drei **Minuten** vor/nach sieben.	It's three _____ to/past seven.
Sie ist kein **Ladendieb**.	She isn't a _____ .
Sie sind keine **Diebe**.	They aren't _____ .
Ich **glaube** nicht, was er sagt.	I don't _____ what he says.
Ist er tot? Wir brauchen **Beweise**.	Is he dead? We need _____ .
Wo ist die **Polizei**?	Where is the _____ ?
Das ist mir egal.	_ _____ _____ .
Ich brauche einen **anderen** Bleistift.	I need _____ pencil.

6 ▶ **Top secret**

Andy Longfinger ist ein bekannter Dieb. Er hat wieder etwas auf dem Kerbholz, weswegen die Polizei hinter ihm her ist. Sein Komplize, der Ganove Lefty, lässt ihm eine Nachricht zukommen, die zwischen Wörtern, die mit Einkaufen oder mit Essen zu tun haben, versteckt sind. Suche diese Wörter heraus, dann weißt du, wie die Nachricht lautet. Schreibe die Wörter in zwei Listen zusammen und mache aus jeder Liste ein network.

money • Dear • **cake** • buy • oranges • Andy • price • ice-cream • meet • shop • tea • customer • me • chips • behind • supermarket • the • lunch • school • pay • at • breakfast • penny • ten • **food** • this • evening • pence • be • eat • careful • pound • the • drink • cheap • expensive • police • dinner • are • **shopping** • looking • assistant • for • sandwich • you • department store • Lefty

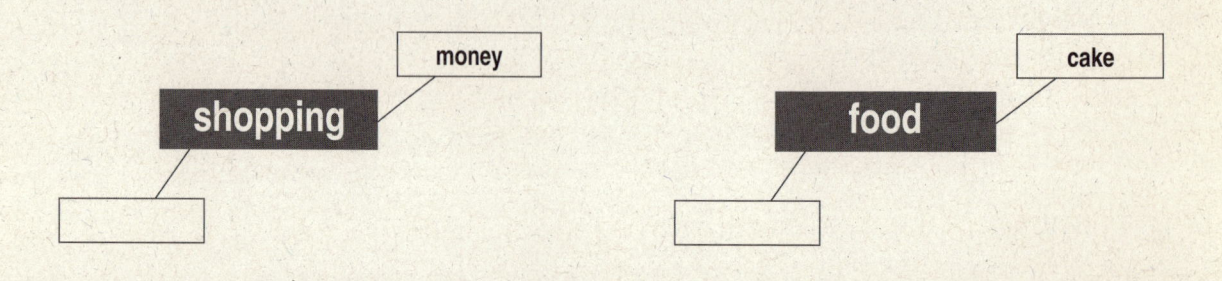

shopping — money

food — cake

To Andy Longfinger: *Dear* _____

7 ▶ Clothes bingo

Bingo ist ein beliebtes englisches Glücksspiel. Unser 'clothes bingo' ist daran angelehnt. Du kannst es mit Freunden oder in der Klasse spielen. Suche vorher aus der Wortschlange 'clothes words' und trage sie x-beliebig im untenstehenden Raster ein. Dann wird ein 'Caller' gewählt, der langsam seine 'clothes words' vorliest. Streiche die Wörter durch, die du eingetragen hast. Wer zuerst eine Spalte oder eine Zeile vollständig hat, ruft Bingo und ist der Gewinner/die Gewinnerin.

Word snake

BIKINIREDSWEATSHIRTBLOUSECLOTHESDRESSTRYONSOCKSTROUSERSSKIRTSHIRTARTANSHOESTARTANNICEPRETTYBLACKJACKETSKIRTBLUESHORTSWHITEGREENLONGSHORTCHILDREN'SCLOTHESSWIMSUITFASHIONSHOEUNIFORMSCARFCLEANDIRTYWASHSWIMMINGTRUNKSBIGWOMEN'SCLOTHESSMALLTAKEOFFLIKENEWOLDBUYNEED

(grid with: wash, clothes, skirt, bikini)

8 ▶ Network

Erweitere dieses Netz mit 'clothes words' aus der Wortschlange. Du kannst auch andere Wörter hinzufügen. Tipp: Schreibt die Wörter auf Vocab cards. So kannst du am besten zusammenstellen, was zusammenpasst.

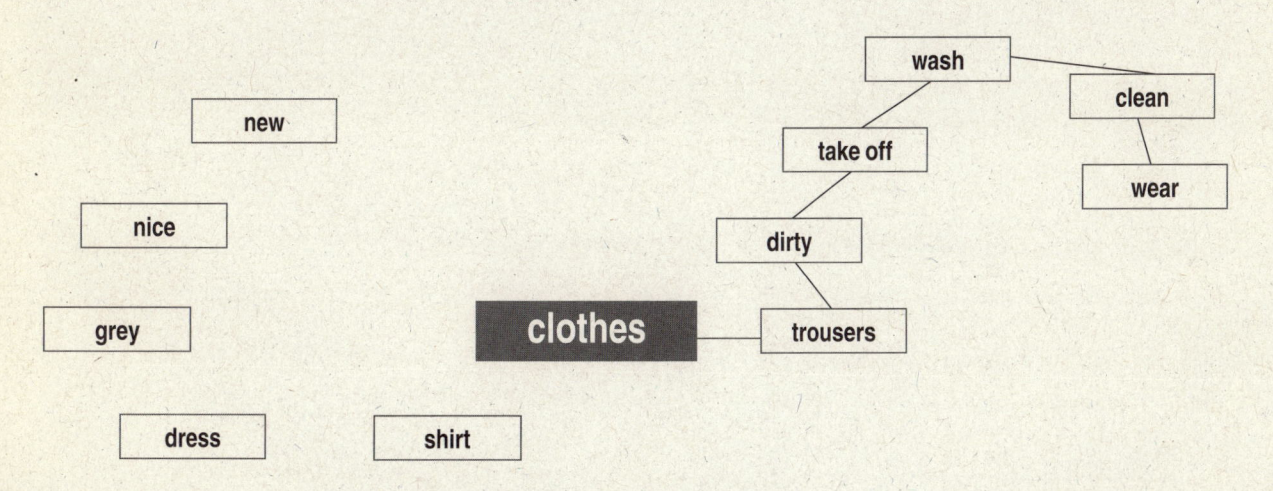

Network around **clothes**:
- new
- nice
- grey
- dress
- shirt
- trousers — dirty — take off — wash — clean — wear

▶ Now you

What are you wearing today? Have you got new clothes?

_____
_____
_____

7 A trip to the zoo

▶ **New words in combinations 7/1** p. 104 - p. 107/A4

einen **Ausflug** nach Chester machen	make a/go on a _____ to Chester
in einen **Zoo** in der Nähe der Stadt gehen	go to a _____ near the town
die **Patenschaft** für Tiere im Zoo **übernehmen**	_____ animals in the zoo
Tiere lieben	love _____
ein großer indischer **Elefant**	a big Indian _____
mit **Tigern** in Käfigen arbeiten	work with _____ in cages
in großer **Gefahr** sein	be in great _____
versuchen, gefährdete Tiere zu **retten**	try and _____ animals in danger
Wann **füttern** sie die Tiere?	When do they _____ the animals?
ein kleiner schwarzer **Vogel** in einem Käfig	a small black _____ in a cage
vor den **Löwen** weglaufen	run away from the _____
Affen schlafen nachts auf Bäumen.	_____ sleep in trees at night.
Was fressen **Giraffen**?	What do _____ eat?
zuerst zu den **Zebras** gehen	go to the _____ first
Trundle ist eine **faule** Schildkröte.	Trundle is a _____ tortoise.
die **Pinguine** beobachten	watch the _____
Lass uns zu den **Seelöwen** gehen.	Let's go to the _____ .
Was kostet ein **Kilo** Orangen?	How much is a _____ _____ oranges?
Willst du Schwarz**brot** oder Weiß**brot**?	Do you want brown or white _____ ?
Sie essen freitags kein **Fleisch**.	They don't eat _____ on Fridays.
Zwei Kilo **Tomaten** bitte.	Two kilos of _____ , please.
eine **Banane** wollen/essen	want/eat a _____
ein **Liter** Orangensaft	a _____ ____ orange juice
jeden Tag einen Liter **Milch** trinken	drink a liter of _____ every day
auf der Straße **herumrennen**	_____ _____ in the street
vorn im Klassenzimmer sitzen	sit ___ ___ _____ of the classroom
Wenn Ann in London ist, trifft sie sich mit Pam.	_____ Ann is in London, she meets Pam.
Ich kann dir **im Moment** nicht helfen.	I can't help you ___ ___ _____ .
Zootiere, **zum Beispiel** Löwen	zoo animals – lions, ____ _____
die neue Telefonnummer **herausfinden**	_____ ____ the new phone number
Wie viel Geld hast du?	_____ _____ money have you got?
Wie viele Tiere sind im Zoo?	_____ _____ animals are there in the zoo?
live in Germany	_____ in Germany

▶ **New words in combinations 7/2**　　　　　　　　　　　　　　　　　　　p. 107/A5 - 113/P 16

auf einem kleinem **Bauernhof** arbeiten	work on a small _____
die **Kühe** füttern	feed the _____
auf einer Farm mit 2000 **Schafen** leben	live on a farm with 2000 _____
Die Farm hat 400 Kühe und 2000 **Schweine**.	The farm has got 400 cows and 2000 _____ .
Wo **wohnst** du? – **Auf dem Land**.	Where do you _____ ? – ___ ____ _____ .
Kühe **auf** grünen **Weiden/Wiesen**	cows ____ green _____
Sind deine Hausaufgaben **fertig**?	Is your homework _____ ?
Im Zoo sind nicht **viele** Löwen.	There aren't _____ lions in the zoo.
Das Tier **sieht wie** ein Vogel **aus**.	The animal _____ _____ a bird.
Mach eine Liste, **bevor** du einkaufen gehst.	Make a list _____ you go shopping.
große/kleine/rote **Ohren** haben	have big/small/red _____
deine **Augen** öffnen/schließen	open/close your _____
Gehen wir doch nach Hause. – Ja, **in Ordnung**.	Let's go home. – ____ _____ .
Es ist kein **echter** Tiger!	It isn't a _____ tiger.
Roboter können viele Arbeiten verrichten.	_____ can do a lot of jobs.
einen Namen/einen Ort **raten/erraten**	_____ a name/a place
Sie isst kein Fleisch. Sie ist **Vegetarierin**.	She doesn't eat meat. She's a _____ .
mehr/weitere Wörter/Sätze/Auskünfte	_____ words/sentences/information

1 ▶ Fast reading game with a partner

Wie schnell kannst du mit einem Partner/einer Partnerin die kurzen Dialoge lesen?
Der Buchstabe x wird durch a, e, i, o oder u ersetzt.

Miss Hunt　Why dx yxx thxnk zxxs xrx txrrxblx fxr thx xnxmxls?
Jenny　　　Bxcxxsx thxy'rx xn cxgxs xnd cxn't rxn xrxxnd.

Assistant　Mxy I hxlp yxx?
Customer　Nx, thxnk yxx, I'm jxst lxxkxng.

Boy　　　　Dx yxx lxkx yxxr jxb xt thx zxx?
Zoo keeper　Yxs, vxry mxch, bxcxxsx wx try xnd sxvx xnxmxls xn dxngxr.

Policeman　Thx xthxr gxrl xs x shxplxftxr,
　　　　　　txx? Hxvx yxx gxt prxxf?
Assistant　Wxll, I thxnk thx twx xrx
　　　　　　wxrkxng txgxthxr.

Teacher　Rxxd thx nxxt sxntxnce plxxsx, Sita.
Sita　　　Sxrry, I cxn't fxnd xt. Whxt pxgx xrx wx xn?

Fritz　Why dx pxxplx txkx thxngs tx Xxfxm shxps?
Ben　　Bxcxxsx thxy'vx gxt lxts xf xld clxthxs,
　　　 txys xnd xthxr thxngs, xnd thxy dxn't nxxd thxm.

Man　　I'vx gxt prxblxms wxth thx cxmpxtxr.
Girl　　Sxrry, Dxd, bxt I cxn't hxlp yxx xt thx mxmxnt.

Just for fun

When have elephants got sixteen feet? –
When there are four of them.

New words in combinations 7/3
p.114 - 115

ein **Kostüm** tragen/ausziehen/waschen	wear/take off/wash a _____
Sie ist **die beste** Lehrerin hier.	She's ____ _____ teacher here.
Hallo. Ich bin euer **Diskjockey** heute Abend.	Hi. I'm your _____ tonight.
Zwei **Eintrittskarten** für Kinder bitte.	Two children's _____ , please.
Der erste **Preis** für das beste Foto geht an Pat.	The first _____ for the best photo goes to Pat.
ein **langsames** Auto	a _____ car
ganz allein nachts (zu Fuß) heimgehen	go home ____ _____ at night
Wer ist da? – **Ich bin es** – Mike.	Who's there? – ____ ____ – Mike.
Was **hälst** du **von** dem neuen Lehrer?	What do you _____ ____ the new teacher?
Warum lachen und **jubeln** die Kinder?	Why are all kids laughing and _____ ?

2 ▶ Merlin's zoo
Merlin der Zauberer hat in seinem Zoo jeweils mehrere Tiere in ein einziges Tier verzaubert. Kannst du aus den englischen Tiernamen neue Namen für diese Tiere 'zaubern', z.B. 'monfibit' für das erste Tier?

1 _____ 3 _____ 5 _____

2 _____ 4 _____ 6 _____

3 ▶ Was sagst du, wenn ...

du jemanden ansprechen willst?	*Excuse me.*
du wissen willst, was vor sich geht?	
du das Telefon benutzen willst?	
du willst, dass jemand aufpassen soll?	
du wissen willst, was eine CD kostet?	
du wissen willst, wie spät es ist?	
du jemandem deine Hilfe anbieten willst?	

4 ▶ At a zoo, on a farm, pets

This is a puzzle with numbers. The numbers stand for letters: 1 = M, 2 = O, 3 = N, etc.
Find the words and maybe draw pictures.

1	2	3	4	5	6	7	8	9	10	11	12	13	14	15	16	17	18	19	20	21	22	23	24
M	O	N	K	E	Y																		

5 ▶ My favourite animal

Draw a picture of your favourite animal or find a photo in a magazine and put it here.
Then write some sentences or a short story about it.

Put your picture here.

thirty-seven

6 ▶ The fourth word

1	little	• cheap
	much	• _____
2	go	• come
	give	• _____
3	a, b, c	• spell
	1, 2, 3	• _____
4	TV	• watch
	radio	• _____

5	people	• walk
	birds	• _____
6	listen	• to
	wait	• _____
7	story	• read
	song	• _____
8	bed	• bedroom
	car	•

9	dream	• about
	laugh	• _____
10	drink	• orange juice
	_____	• sandwiches
11	look at	• pictures
	_____	• games
12	write with	• a pencil
	_____	• a bench

7 ▶ ai, au, ea, ee, ie, oa, oo, ou
Fill in the missing letters and complete the words.

1 sl ___ p	11 cant ___ n	21 cupb ___ rd	31 m ___ t
2 pr ___ f	12 ch ___ p	22 of c ___ rse	32 m ___ t
3 f ___ rteen	13 d ___ r	23 dr ___ m	33 b ___ ch
4 bl ___ se	14 d ___ r	24 fav ___ rite	34 r ___ m
5 col ___ r	15 p ___ r	25 gr ___ p	35 ag ___ n
6 bel ___ ve	16 fr ___ nd	26 gr ___ n	36 f ___ d
7 t ___	17 ___ nt	27 h ___ r	37 f ___ d
8 t ___	18 rest ___ rant	28 h ___ se	38 ch ___ r
9 bec ___ se	19 th ___ f	29 qu ___ t	39 ___ t
10 b ___ rd	20 gr ___ t	30 l ___ gh	40 ___ t

Just for fun

Teacher Your text about 'My dog' is word for word like your brother's text.
Pupil I know. It's the same dog.

Englishman Look, there's an English cow.
German Oh no, it must be a German cow.
Scotsman You're both wrong. It's a Scottish cow. Look, it's got bagpipes.

What's the difference between a cow and a baby?
A cow drinks water and makes milk. A baby drinks milk and makes water.

English G 2000 • Wordmaster A1 • Schlüssel

Welcome **Crossword puzzle**
Across: 1 *spell* 2 Germany 4 fine 6 mum 7 name 9 too 11 little
Down: 1 speak 3 morning 4 from 5 count 8 English 10 old

Unit 1 1▶ **Questions, questions**
Hello. What's your name? • Where are you from? • Are you two brother and sister? • What colour is your school bag? • Is Ashton a village near Chester? • How old are you? • Is Tom German or English? • Where's my English book? • Is your sister in Form 9? • Are Tom and Joe friends? • Where's your classroom? • What's 'tortoise' in German?

2▶ **Word mix**
1 Debbie and Nick are my new friends. 2 Debbie and Nick are brother and sister.
3 The twins are in my form. 4 How old are your new friends? 5 Where are they from?
6 Jenny and Sita aren't sisters. 7 The two girls aren't in my form.

4▶ **The fourth word**
1 sister 2 village 3 English 4 colour 5 letters 6 his

Unit 2 1▶ **Find the right way**
1 *Look. The budgie isn't in its cage. Where is it?* 2 I can't see the rabbit. It isn't in the garden.
3 A hamster is a nice pet for kids. 4 Here's a photo of my sister with her cat. 5 Is your dog a 'he' or a 'she'? 6 Jenny is with her Grandma in Halle. 7 How old is your dog? 8 The name of the happy little rabbit is Sue. 9 Debbie and Nick are in the garden. 10 Is Ben home from school? 11 I'm Paul. And who are you? 12 My uncle is a nurse.

2▶ **Where's my pullover?**
1 *exercise* 2 count 3 complete 4 number 5 school 6 page 7 tortoise 8 Indian
→ cupboard

3▶ **Picture puzzle**
Across: 1 bag 2 rubber 5 pen 6 tortoise 8 cat 9 dog 10 budgie 11 ruler
12 hamster
Down: 1 board 3 biro 4 goldfish 5 pencil 7 rabbit

5▶ **Fast reading game**
answer all the questions, answer the phone, make a cage for the hamster, make sentences, wash the dirty pullover again, look at the pictures on page 25, look at the notice board, write words and numbers, read a story about a girl and her little white rabbit, read the sentence again, swap a ruler for a rubber, swap a pullover for a T-shirt, go home together, go to the new restaurant

6▶ **Positive or negative?**
Positive: clever, cool, fine, funny, good, happy, lucky, married, new, nice, quiet, right
Negative: boring, dead, divorced, late, lovely, old, poor, silly, wrong

Unit 3 1▶ **Black and white**
Across: 2 *black* 4 here 6 downstairs 10 Mrs 11 question 13 sister 14 no 15 hear
Down: 1 grandma 3 wrong 5 girlfriend 7 over 8 clever 9 aunt 12 wife

2▶ **Word mix**
I think Jenny is washing the dishes. • The kids are packing for the weekend. • Ben is doing his English homework in his room. • Can you help Ben with this exercise, please? • Sorry, I can't help you, I haven't got time.

3▶ **What can you do?**
go to the toilet • listen to the radio • watch TV • write a letter • sit on a chair • use a rubber • wait for us in the car • play a game • read in bed • work in the kitchen • draw a dream house

4▶ **At, in, on, to?**
1 at 2 to 3 to 4 at 5 on 6 at 7 on 8 in 9 on 10 on 11 at 12 to 13 on 14 at

5▶ **Odd word out**
1 *biro* 2 my 3 hall 4 pet 5 house 6 three 7 red 8 swap

Unit 4 1▶ **Missing letters**
1 letter 2 room 3 picture 4 tree 5 story 6 garden 7 game 8 window
9 video 10 name 11 people 12 song

2▶ **Word mix**
Put the orange juice here, please. • Can you come back at three o'clock? •
I'm looking for a birthday present for my mum. • A new bike is a great birthday
present. • I'm looking for a cheap bookshelf. • He's dreaming about a nice weekend
in Ashton. • Mrs Keller is writing a book about Chester. • She's a divorced woman
with three small children. • Let's sit on this bench under the tree. • The garage is
next to the restaurant. • Our garden is between two big houses. • What time is it
now, please?

3▶ **Let's talk about people**
Group 1: husband, wife, girlfriend, girl, boy, cousin, partner, mother, brother, uncle,
boyfriend, aunt, man, family, sister, teacher, grandpa, father, grandma, woman,
twins
Group 2: happy, married, British, big, Indian, clever, old, silly, little, boring, dead, small,
poor, nice, quiet, funny, lucky

4▶ **Read, say and write**
Across: 4 again 5 women 6 cousin 8 cupboard 12 downstairs 13 car 14 climb
15 calendar 16 laugh 17 benches
Down: 1 dance 2 restaurant 3 upstairs 7 sandwich 9 scarves 10 candle 11 picture

5▶ **This and that**
1 *white* 2 old 3 there 4 down 5 then 6 no 7 go 8 play 9 drink 10 night
11 tomorrow 12 women 13 wives 14 mother 15 sisters 16 children

Unit 5 1▶ **The fourth word**
1 lunch 2 wash 3 finish 4 canteen 5 at night 6 wife

2▶ **All good things come in threes**
1 j g • 2 h c • 3 n d • 4 a f • 5 g b • 6 c a • 7 b o • 8 k m • 9 d k • 10 e i •
11 l e • 12 i j • 13 f l • 14 m h • 15 o n

3▶ **A new letter – a new word**
1 bag 2 Thank 3 bed 4 song 5 Tell 6 Fill 7 cake 8 late

4▶ **Comb puzzle**
Down: 1 girls 2 after 3 dirty 4 order 5 house 6 right; *Across:* grandmother

5▶ **Find the right way**
It's not funny, so don't laugh. • Open your books at page 71. • Let's swap stickers. • Can
you answer all the questions? • Is this your pencil-case? • The two girls are twins. •
More information is on the notice board. • Take this box downstairs. • *Write your name
on your test.* • Put the film in the video recorder. • Sit down on the bench. • Make
your bed after breakfast. • What's for dinner today? • Can you speak English? •
Collect information about your town. • Lessons start at eight in our school.

6▶ **Picture puzzle**
Across: 2 desk 3 bookshelf 4 bench 6 picture 9 calendar 10 door 11 window
Down: 1 basket 3 bin 4 box 5 cupboard 7 table 8 chair

7▶ **Missing letters**
1 dr*aw*/*away* 2 cous*in*/*information* 3 phone/next 4 mon*th*/*th*ink 5 wom*an*/*an*swer
6 be*fore*/*read* 7 t*ime*/*meet* 8 d*ear*/*around* 9 fin*ish*/*shopping* 10 lo*ve*/*ve*ry
11 ha*te*/*te*am 12 less*on*/*only* 13 bi*ro*/*room* 14 tr*ouble*/*learn* 15 tab*le*/*le*tter

8▶ **Word mix**
1 Haven't you got a new timetable? 2 Do your friends collect stamps, too?
3 Is maths your favourite subject? 4 Is there a notice board at your school?
5 When's the lunch break? 6 Can you buy lunch in the school canteen?

9▶ **Sound check**
1 club 2 lunch 3 canteen 4 lesson 5 sport 6 assembly 7 break

10▶ **Making new words**
4 timetable 5 girlfriend 6 supermarket 7 bookshelf 8 living-room 9 football
10 notice board 11 goldfish 12 football team 13 felt-tip 14 English teacher

15 lunch break   16 bedroom   17 drama group   18 school uniform   19 stamp club
20 school subject   21 weekend

11 ▶ **Four-letter words**
1 page   2 cage   3 name   4 date   5 game   6 late   7 hate   8 take

12 ▶ **Race against time**
1 Please do your homework at home.   2 Tidy up the classroom after your lesson.
3 Don't speak German in the English lesson.   4 Please open your books at page 85.
5 Put the words in the right order.   6 Can I read the next sentence?   7 Can I open the window, please?   8 What's 'Fehler' in English?

13 ▶ **Words in a spider's web**
1 blue   2 come   3 home   4 live   5 time   6 here   7 make   8 late   9 June   10 shoe
11 take   12 fine   13 give   14 wife   15 line   16 like   17 mice   18 ride

Unit 6

1 ▶ **Plurals**
boxes, prices, wives, halves, mice, shelves, benches, matches, men, children, cities, watches, hobbies, women

2 ▶ **One word – ten things**
the radio, a special shop, your bike, that toy, your name, fashion, a drama class, the letter, your homework, his bed

3 ▶ **Odd word out**
man, questionnaire, calendar, only

4 ▶ **Words looking for friends**
information, clothes, toys, a word, a song, a letter, bed, lunch, stamps, a video, English, a window, your room, a job, a swimming-pool, a tree, a sentence, a story

5 ▶ **Opposites and similar words**
before: – , after; *silly:* stupid, clever; *like:* love, hate; *children:* kids, – ; *long:* – , short; *wrong:* – , right; *left:* – , right; *in front of:* – , behind; *yes:* – , no; *always:* usually, never; *small:* little, big; *nice:* pretty, – ; *great:* super, – ; *clean:* – , dirty; *upstairs:* – , downstairs; *quick:* – , slow; *bad:* terrible, good; *new:* – , old; *cheap:* – , expensive

6 ▶ **Top secret**
Shopping: money, buy, price, shop, customer, supermarket, pay, penny, pence, pound, cheap, expensive, assistant, department store.
Food: cake, oranges, ice-cream, tea, chips, lunch, breakfast, eat, drink, dinner, sandwich.

Dear Andy,
Meet me behind the school at ten this evening. Be careful, the police are looking for you.
    Lefty

Unit 7

1 ▶ **Fast reading game with a partner**

Miss Hunt   Why do you think zoos are terrible for the animals?
Jenny   Because they're are in cages and can't run around.

Assistant   May I help you?
Customer   No, thank you, I'm just looking.

Boy   Do you like your jobs at the zoo?
Zoo keeper   Yes, very much, because we try and save animals in danger.

Teacher   Read the next sentence please, Sita.
Sita   Sorry, I can't find it. What page are we on?

Policeman   The other girl is a shoplifter, too? Have you got proof?
Assistant   Well, I think the two are working together.

Fritz   Why do people take things to Oxfam shops?
Ben   Because they've got lots of old clothes, toys and other things, and they don't need them.

Man   I've got problems with the computer.
Girl   Sorry, Dad, but I can't help you at the moment.

2 ▶ **Merlin's zoo**
1 monfibit, …   2 eletomo, …   3 girtigon, …   4 dopenird, …   5 cashow, …   6 lizebrig, …

3 ▶ **Was sagst du, wenn …**
Excuse me. • What's happening? • May I use the phone, please? • Be careful. • How much is this CD? • What time is it, please? • May I help you?

4 ▶ **At a zoo, on a farm, pets**

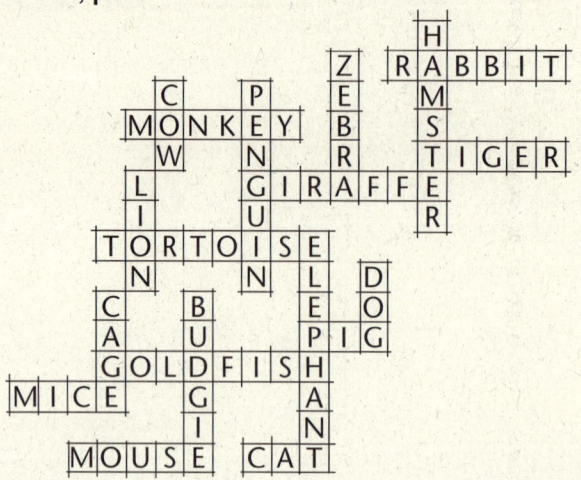

```
                    H
          Z       R A B B I T
          E       A
      C   P       M
    M O N K E Y   S
      W   N       T I G E R
      L   G I R A F F E
      I   U       E
    T O R T O I S E
      N   N   L   D
    C     B   E   O
    A     U   P I G
  G O L D F I S H
  M I C E G     A
    A     I     N
    M O U S E   C A T
```

6 ▶ **The fourth word**
1 expensive   2 take   3 count   4 listen (to)   5 fly   6 for   7 sing   8 garage   9 at   10 eat
11 play   12 sit on

7 ▶ **ai, au, ea, ee, ie, oa, oo, ou**
1 sleep   2 proof   3 fourteen   4 blouse   5 colour   6 believe   7/8 tea/too   9 because
10 board   11 canteen   12 cheap   13/14 door/dear   15 poor   16 friend   17 aunt
18 restaurant   19 thief   20 great   21 cupboard   22 of course   23 dream   24 favourite
25 group   26 green   27 hour   28 house   29 quiet   30 laugh   31/32 meat/meet
33 beach   34 room   35 again   36/37 food/feed   38 chair   39/40 eat/out

Unit 8 1 ▶ **Play – do – go**
At English schools <u>pupils</u> can <u>play</u> football, <u>hockey/…</u> and <u>volleyball/…</u> . The children can <u>do</u> drama and <u>judo/…</u>, too. In the summer kids <u>go</u> swimming or <u>fishing/…</u> . At the weekend many English children <u>go</u> <u>dancing</u> at a disco.
At German schools we can <u>play …, do …, go …</u> .

2 ▶ **Opposites – a crossword puzzle**
Across: 5 daughter   6 sister   7 downstairs   8 married   9 walk   10 good
Down: 1 *his*   2 dog   3 answer   4 girlfriend   6 in front of   7 over   11 pm

3 ▶ **Word mix**
Do your parents drive you to school? • There's so much traffic here in the morning. • We always go on holiday in the summer. • Has Sita got any plans for next week? • There's a message for you from your mum. • I'm not going to invite Miss Hunt to my party.

4 ▶ **Sound check**
[dʒ] giraffe, orange, gym, sandwich, judo, large, vegetarian, budgie, message
[ʃ]   shout, delcious, lunch, fashion, Turkish, finished, sheep, beach

5 ▶ **Which words go together?**
clean the bathroom; make invitation cards; have a party; work in the kitchen; act in a play; wait in the car; collect words; carry the shopping bag; want a new dress; drive a bus

6 ▶ **So many 'tos'**
1 *an*   2 vor   3 in   4 bis   5 nach   6 mit   7 in(s)   8 bis

7 ▶ **Odd word out**
1 sandals   2 chips   3 CD shop   4 lion   5 France   6 but   7 country   8 calendar

8 ▶ **Puzzle it out**
today; record; uncle; nothing; December; letter; exercises

8 Fun in the holidays

▶ **New words in combinations 8/1** p. 118 - p. 120/A3

viel **Spaß** haben	have lots of _____
Ferien sind toll.	_____ are great.
Ich mag **Sommer**tage.	I like _____ days.
eine **kostenlose** Eintrittskarte	a _____ ticket
Ich mag **Kajakfahren** und **Angeln**.	I love _____ and _____.
Mein Lieblingssport ist **Schwimmen**.	My favourite sport is _____.
Tom **fährt** nicht zur Schule mit seinem Auto.	Tom doesn't _____ to school with his car.
London hat drei **Flughäfen**.	London has got three _____.
In Chester ist heute viel **Verkehr**.	There's lots of _____ in Chester today.
ein schrecklicher **Unfall**	a terrible _____
Schau, ein **Flugzeug** aus Deutschland!	Look, a _____ from Germany!
Wir müssen eine **Meile** laufen.	We must run one _____.
eine **Nachricht** für Ben	a _____ for Ben
Debbie **hat Hunger** und **Durst**.	Debbie ___ _____ and _____.
Fahrt nicht so **schnell**.	Don't drive so _____.
Wir haben einen **großen** Garten.	We've got a _____ garden.
Ich brauche **Salz** für meine Pommes frites.	I need _____ for my chips.
ein **köstlicher** Kuchen	a _____ cake

1 ▶ Play – do – go
Complete the sentences with play, do, go and some 'activity words'.

At Englisch schools _____ can _____ football, _____ and _____. The

children can _____ drama and _____, too. In the summer kids _____ swimming or _____.

At the weekend many English children _____ _____ at a disco.

At German schools we can _____.

After school kids at my school sometimes _____.

▶ **Now you**
What are your favourite activities. Where can you do them?

_____

_____

_____

thirty-nine

New words in combinations 8/2

p.121/A4 - p. 122/A8

Lasst uns in Chester **umher**gehen.	Let's _____ around Chester.
Ich mag London nicht. Es ist so **laut**.	I don't like London. It's so _____ .
Gibt es hier (**irgendwelche**) gute CDs?	_____ _____ _____ good CDs here?
Es gibt **keine** guten CDs hier.	There are _____ _____ good CDs here.
Mein Vater hat viele alte **Schallplatten**.	My father has got lots of old _____ .
Ist das die **Straße** nach Ashton?	Is this the _____ to Ashton?
ein **türkisches** Mädchen	a _____ girl
Ich höre manchmal **klassische** Musik.	I sometimes listen to _____ music.
Bitte **schreit** hier nicht.	Please don't _____ here.
Vorsicht Nick – ein Auto!	_____ _____ Nick – a car!
Warum **kochen** wir nicht unser Lieblingsessen?	Why don't we _____ our favourite food?
Ich mag **Lamm** mit **Kartoffeln**.	I like _____ with _____ .
Pläne für den Urlaub haben	have _____ for the holidays
Im Sommer werden wir unsere Tante **besuchen**.	We're going to _____ our aunt in the summer.
noch ein Tag **bis** zu meinem Geburtstag	one more day _____ my birthday

2 ▶ Opposites – a crossword puzzle

Look at the solutions (Lösungen) in the crossword puzzle and then find the missing clues (Hinweise).

```
         1       2       3               4
         H       C       Q               B
         E       A       U       5       
                                 S       O       N
    6
    B    R       O       T       H       E       R
    E                    S                       F
    H            7
                 U       P       S       T       A       I       R       S
    I            N               I                       I
                 8
    N            D       I       V       O       R       C       E       D
    D            E               N                       N
                 9
                 R       U       N       10      11
                                         B       A       D
                                                 M
```

Across 5 ▶◀ _____
        6 ▶◀ _____
        7 ▶◀ _____
        8 ▶◀ _____
        9 ▶◀ _____
        10 ▶◀ _____

Down 1 ▶◀ *his*
      2 ▶◀ _____
      3 ▶◀ _____
      4 ▶◀ _____
      6 ▶◀ _____
      7 ▶◀ _____
      11 ▶◀ _____

▶ **New words in combinations 8/3**   p. 123/A9 - p. 129

eine nette **Person**	a nice _____
um die **Welt** fliegen	fly around the _____
Morgen werde ich zu Hause **bleiben**.	I'm going to _____ at home tomorrow.
Milch und **Kakao**	milk and _____
Die Kinder spielen auf dem **Schulhof**.	The children are playing in the _____.
Wirf den Ball in die **Luft** und renne weg.	_____ the ball into the ____ and run away.
Der Ball wird auf den Boden **fallen**.	The ball is going to _____ on the floor.
Ist Marmalade **draußen** oder **drinnen**?	Is Marmalade _____ or _____ ?
Die Leute **klatschen** und **pfeifen**.	The people are _____ and _____ .
Lasst uns Miss Hunt zu unserer Party **einladen**.	Let's _____ Miss Hunt to our party.
Werdet ihr nach Chester fahren? – Ich **hoffe** es.	Are you going to go to Chester? – I _____ so.
Lieber Nick, alles ist in Ornung. **Deine** Debbie	Dear Nick, Everything is all right. _____ Debbie

3 ▶ **Word mix**
Put the words in the right order and make sentences.

to you your **drive** parents school? Do   _____

the so There's in here **traffic** much morning.   _____

summer. We always on holiday in go the   _____

week? for next Sita any Has got **plans**   _____

message from mum. There's you a for your   _____

I'm not party. my to Miss Hunt going **invite** to   _____

4 ▶ **Sound check**
Match the sounds and words.

		5 ▶ **Which words go together?**	
giraffe	fashion	clean	the shopping bag
orange	large	make	in the kitchen
shout	Turkish	have	the bathroom
delicious	finished	work	more words
lunch	vegetarian	act	invitation cards
gym	budgie	wait	a party
collect	sheep	collect	a new dress
sandwich	beach	carry	a bus
judo	message	want	in a play
		drive	in the car

[dʒ] [ʃ]

giraffe — fashion (line to [dʒ])
sandwich — beach (line to [ʃ])

make — invitation cards

6 ▶ So many 'tos'

Find the right German word (an, bis, in, mit, nach, vor) for the word 'to' in the following sentences.

1 I must write a letter **to** my grandma. _an_
2 It's twenty **to** three. _vor_
3 Welcome **to** Berlin, Ben. _in_
4 The lesson is from 9.45 **to** 10.30. _bis_
5 Let's go **to** London tomorrow. _nach_
6 Nick, please don't talk **to** Ben. _mit_
7 We're going **to** the cinema. _in_
8 School is from Monday **to** Friday. _bis_

7 ▶ Odd word out

1 shirt, blouse, shorts, sandals
2 chips, ice-cream, cake, biscuit
3 books, records, CD shop, CDs
4 sheep, lion, pig, cow
5 English, France, Turkish, Indian
6 behind, to, but, from
7 city, country, town, village
8 day, calendar, month, week

1 _sandals_   5 _France_
2 _chips_   6 _but_
3 _CD shop_   7 _country_
4 _lion_   8 _calendar_

8 ▶ Puzzle it out (Find es heraus)

Make words with the 'word parts' in the box below.

> ber • ci • cle • cem • cord • day • de • er • ex • let • no • re • ses • ter • thing • to • un

not tomorrow — _today_
something you can listen to — _record_
an aunt's husband — _uncle_
not everything — _nothing_
the twelfth month — _December_
'a' for example — _letter_
you do them in English lessons — _exercises_

9 ▶ Networking

a *Try and find lots of words for the prepositions.*

- **next** — week, ...
- **behind** — the garden, ...
- **under** — the cupboard, ...
- **at** — school, ...

b *Now make sentences.*

Next week I'm going to visit some friends.

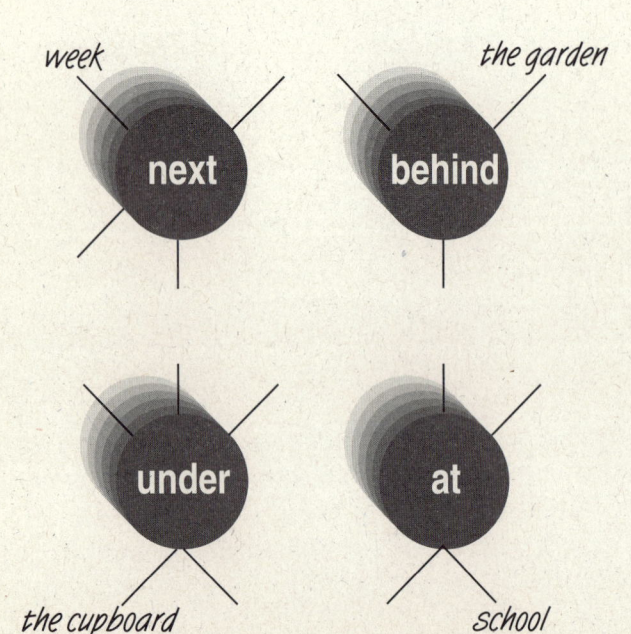

10 ▶ **Activity: My English class in 19 ...**

> *Hier kannst du ein Bild von deiner Klasse mit eurem Englischlehrer oder eurer Englischlehrerin einkleben.*
>
> *Tipp: Lege Klarsichtfolie auf das Bild und zeichne darauf die Umrisse deiner Mitschüler/innen und deines Lehrers oder deiner Lehrerin mit einem wasserunlöslichen Filzstift.*
> *Schreibe Nummern in die Umrisse.*
> *Dann klebst du das Foto und die Folie so ein, dass du die Folie über dem Foto herunterklappen kannst.*
> *Zum Schluss trägst du die Namen ein.*
> *Natürlich können auch alle unterschreiben. Das ist viel persönlicher.*

1 _____	13 _____	25 _____
2 _____	14 _____	26 _____
3 _____	15 _____	27 _____
4 _____	16 _____	28 _____
5 _____	17 _____	29 _____
6 _____	18 _____	30 _____
7 _____	19 _____	31 _____
8 _____	20 _____	32 _____
9 _____	21 _____	33 _____
10 _____	22 _____	34 _____
11 _____	23 _____	35 _____
12 _____	24 _____	36 _____

Write some sentences about you, your classmates and your teacher. You can start like this:
I'm number ... . The boy/girl behind me ... . He's/She's my friend. We live in the same street. We ...

_____

_____

_____

_____

_____

_____

_____

_____

Vocab cards **Kopiervorlage**

Male die ☺ auf der Vorderseite der Karten farbig aus, damit die Karten nicht durcheinander geraten und du leicht Ordnung halten kannst.

English G 2000 • Wordmaster A1 • Schlüssel

Welcome **Crossword puzzle**
Across: 1 *spell* 2 Germany 4 fine 6 mum 7 name 9 too 11 little
Down: 1 speak 3 morning 4 from 5 count 8 English 10 old

Unit 1 1▶ **Questions, questions**
Hello. What's your name? • Where are you from? • Are you two brother and sister? • What colour is your school bag? • Is Ashton a village near Chester? • *How old are you?* • Is Tom German or English? • Where's my English book? • Is your sister in Form 9? • Are Tom and Joe friends? • Where's your classroom? • What's 'tortoise' in German?

2▶ **Word mix**
1 Debbie and Nick are my new friends. 2 Debbie and Nick are brother and sister. 3 The twins are in my form. 4 How old are your new friends? 5 Where are they from? 6 Jenny and Sita aren't sisters. 7 The two girls aren't in my form.

4▶ **The fourth word**
1 sister 2 village 3 English 4 colour 5 letters 6 his

Unit 2 1▶ **Find the right way**
1 *Look. The budgie isn't in its cage. Where is it?* 2 I can't see the rabbit. It isn't in the garden. 3 A hamster is a nice pet for kids. 4 Here's a photo of my sister with her cat. 5 Is your dog a 'he' or a 'she'? 6 Jenny is with her Grandma in Halle. 7 How old is your dog? 8 The name of the happy little rabbit is Sue. 9 Debbie and Nick are in the garden. 10 Is Ben home from school? 11 I'm Paul. And who are you? 12 My uncle is a nurse.

2▶ **Where's my pullover?**
1 *exercise* 2 count 3 complete 4 number 5 school 6 page 7 tortoise 8 Indian
→ cupboard

3▶ **Picture puzzle**
Across: 1 bag 2 rubber 5 pen 6 tortoise 8 cat 9 dog 10 budgie 11 ruler 12 hamster
Down: 1 board 3 biro 4 goldfish 5 pencil 7 rabbit

5▶ **Fast reading game**
answer all the questions, answer the phone, make a cage for the hamster, make sentences, wash the dirty pullover again, look at the pictures on page 25, look at the notice board, write words and numbers, read a story about a girl and her little white rabbit, read the sentence again, swap a ruler for a rubber, swap a pullover for a T-shirt, go home together, go to the new restaurant

6▶ **Positive or negative?**
Positive: clever, cool, fine, funny, good, happy, lucky, married, new, nice, quiet, right
Negative: boring, dead, divorced, late, lovely, old, poor, silly, wrong

Unit 3 1▶ **Black and white**
Across: 2 *black* 4 here 6 downstairs 10 Mrs 11 question 13 sister 14 no 15 hear
Down: 1 grandma 3 wrong 5 girlfriend 7 over 8 clever 9 aunt 12 wife

2▶ **Word mix**
I think Jenny is washing the dishes. • The kids are packing for the weekend. • Ben is doing his English homework in his room. • Can you help Ben with this exercise, please? • Sorry, I can't help you, I haven't got time.

3▶ **What can you do?**
go to the toilet • listen to the radio • watch TV • write a letter • sit on a chair • use a rubber • wait for us in the car • play a game • read in bed • work in the kitchen • draw a dream house

4▶ **At, in, on, to?**
1 at 2 to 3 to 4 at 5 on 6 at 7 on 8 in 9 on 10 on 11 at 12 to 13 on 14 at

5▶ **Odd word out**
1 *biro* 2 my 3 hall 4 pet 5 house 6 three 7 red 8 swap

1

Unit 4 1▶ **Missing letters**
1 letter 2 room 3 picture 4 tree 5 story 6 garden 7 game 8 window
9 video 10 name 11 people 12 song

2▶ **Word mix**
Put the orange juice here, please. • Can you come back at three o'clock? • I'm looking for a birthday present for my mum. • A new bike is a great birthday present. • I'm looking for a cheap bookshelf. • He's dreaming about a nice weekend in Ashton. • Mrs Keller is writing a book about Chester. • She's a divorced woman with three small children. • Let's sit on this bench under the tree. • The garage is next to the restaurant. • Our garden is between two big houses. • What time is it now, please?

3▶ **Let's talk about people**
Group 1: husband, wife, girlfriend, girl, boy, cousin, partner, mother, brother, uncle, boyfriend, aunt, man, family, sister, teacher, grandpa, father, grandma, woman, twins
Group 2: happy, married, British, big, Indian, clever, old, silly, little, boring, dead, small, poor, nice, quiet, funny, lucky

4▶ **Read, say and write**
Across: 4 again 5 women 6 cousin 8 cupboard 12 downstairs 13 car 14 climb
15 calendar 16 laugh 17 benches
Down: 1 dance 2 restaurant 3 upstairs 7 sandwich 9 scarves 10 candle 11 picture

5▶ **This and that**
1 *white* 2 old 3 there 4 down 5 then 6 no 7 go 8 play 9 drink 10 night
11 tomorrow 12 women 13 wives 14 mother 15 sisters 16 children

Unit 5 1▶ **The fourth word**
1 lunch 2 wash 3 finish 4 canteen 5 at night 6 wife

2▶ **All good things come in threes**
1 j g • 2 h c • 3 n d • 4 a f • 5 g b • 6 c a • 7 b o • 8 k m • 9 d k • 10 e i •
11 l e • 12 i j • 13 f l • 14 m h • 15 o n

3▶ **A new letter – a new word**
1 bag 2 Thank 3 bed 4 song 5 Tell 6 Fill 7 cake 8 late

4▶ **Comb puzzle**
Down: 1 girls 2 after 3 dirty 4 order 5 house 6 right; *Across:* grandmother

5▶ **Find the right way**
It's not funny, so don't laugh. • Open your books at page 71. • Let's swap stickers. • Can you answer all the questions? • Is this your pencil-case? • The two girls are twins. • More information is on the notice board. • Take this box downstairs. • *Write your name on your test.* • Put the film in the video recorder. • Sit down on the bench. • Make your bed after breakfast. • What's for dinner today? • Can you speak English? • Collect information about your town. • Lessons start at eight in our school.

6▶ **Picture puzzle**
Across: 2 desk 3 bookshelf 4 bench 6 picture 9 calendar 10 door 11 window
Down: 1 basket 3 bin 4 box 5 cupboard 7 table 8 chair

7▶ **Missing letters**
1 dr*aw*/*away* 2 cous*in*/*information* 3 pho*ne*/*next* 4 mon*th*/*th*ink 5 wom*an*/*an*swer
6 befo*re*/*read* 7 ti*me*/*me*et 8 de*ar*/*ar*ound 9 fini*sh*/*sh*opping 10 lo*ve*/*ve*ry
11 ha*te*/*te*am 12 less*on*/*on*ly 13 bi*ro*/*ro*om 14 troub*le*/*le*arn 15 tab*le*/*le*tter

8▶ **Word mix**
1 Haven't you got a new timetable? 2 Do your friends collect stamps, too?
3 Is maths your favourite subject? 4 Is there a notice board at your school?
5 When's the lunch break? 6 Can you buy lunch in the school canteen?

9▶ **Sound check**
1 club 2 lunch 3 canteen 4 lesson 5 sport 6 assembly 7 break

10▶ **Making new words**
4 timetable 5 girlfriend 6 supermarket 7 bookshelf 8 living-room 9 football
10 notice board 11 goldfish 12 football team 13 felt-tip 14 English teacher

15 lunch break   16 bedroom   17 drama group   18 school uniform   19 stamp club
20 school subject   21 weekend

11 ▶ Four-letter words
1 page   2 cage   3 name   4 date   5 game   6 late   7 hate   8 take

12 ▶ Race against time
1 Please do your homework at home.   2 Tidy up the classroom after your lesson.
3 Don't speak German in the English lesson.   4 Please open your books at page 85.
5 Put the words in the right order.   6 Can I read the next sentence?   7 Can I open the window, please?   8 What's 'Fehler' in English?

13 ▶ Words in a spider's web
1 blue   2 come   3 home   4 live   5 time   6 here   7 make   8 late   9 June   10 shoe
11 take   12 fine   13 give   14 wife   15 line   16 like   17 mice   18 ride

Unit 6

1 ▶ Plurals
boxes, prices, wives, halves, mice, shelves, benches, matches, men, children, cities, watches, hobbies, women

2 ▶ One word – ten things
the radio, a special shop, your bike, that toy, your name, fashion, a drama class, the letter, your homework, his bed

3 ▶ Odd word out
man, questionnaire, calendar, only

4 ▶ Words looking for friends
information, clothes, toys, a word, a song, a letter, bed, lunch, stamps, a video, English, a window, your room, a job, a swimming-pool, a tree, a sentence, a story

5 ▶ Opposites and similar words
before: – , after; *silly:* stupid, clever; *like:* love, hate; *children:* kids, – ; *long:* – , short; *wrong:* – , right; *left:* – , right; *in front of:* – , behind; *yes:* – , no; *always:* usually, never; *small:* little, big; *nice:* pretty, – ; *great:* super, – ; *clean:* – , dirty; *upstairs:* – , downstairs; *quick:* – , slow; *bad:* terrible, good; *new:* – , old; *cheap:* – , expensive

6 ▶ Top secret
Shopping: money, buy, price, shop, customer, supermarket, pay, penny, pence, pound, cheap, expensive, assistant, department store.
Food: cake, oranges, ice-cream, tea, chips, lunch, breakfast, eat, drink, dinner, sandwich.

Dear Andy,
Meet me behind the school at ten this evening. Be careful, the police are looking for you.
  Lefty

Unit 7

1 ▶ Fast reading game with a partner

Miss Hunt	Why do you think zoos are terrible for the animals?
Jenny	Because they're are in cages and can't run around.
Assistant	May I help you?
Customer	No, thank you, I'm just looking.
Boy	Do you like your jobs at the zoo?
Zoo keeper	Yes, very much, because we try and save animals in danger.
Teacher	Read the next sentence please, Sita.
Sita	Sorry, I can't find it. What page are we on?
Policeman	The other girl is a shoplifter, too? Have you got proof?
Assistant	Well, I think the two are working together.
Fritz	Why do people take things to Oxfam shops?
Ben	Because they've got lots of old clothes, toys and other things, and they don't need them.
Man	I've got problems with the computer.
Girl	Sorry, Dad, but I can't help you at the moment.

2 ▶ Merlin's zoo
1 monfibit, ...   2 eletomo, ...   3 girtigon, ...   4 dopenird, ...   5 cashow, ...   6 lizebrig, ...

3

3 ▶ **Was sagst du, wenn …**
Excuse me. • What's happening? • May I use the phone, please? • Be careful. • How much is this CD? • What time is it, please? • May I help you?

4 ▶ **At a zoo, on a farm, pets**

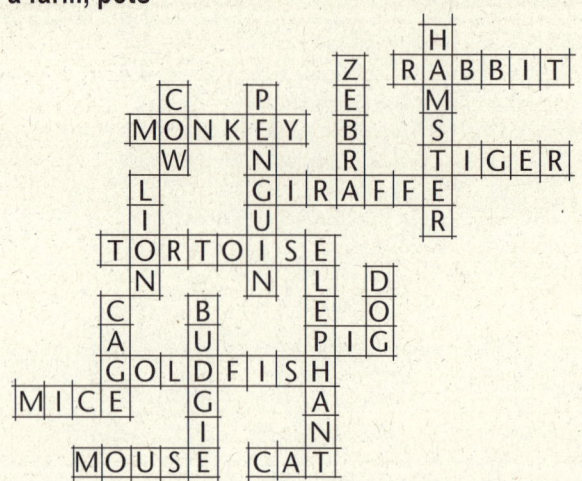

```
              H
          Z R A B B I T
      C   E M
    P E   B S
  M O N K E Y T I G E R
    W N   R
  L I   G I R A F F E
    T O R T O I S E
    N   N   D
  C B     E O G
  A U     P I G
  G O L D F I S H
M I C E   G   A
    G     N
  M O U S E   C A T
```

6 ▶ **The fourth word**
1 expensive   2 take   3 count   4 listen (to)   5 fly   6 for   7 sing   8 garage   9 at   10 eat   11 play   12 sit on

7 ▶ **ai, au, ea, ee, ie, oa, oo, ou**
1 sleep   2 proof   3 fourteen   4 blouse   5 colour   6 believe   7/8 tea/too   9 because   10 board   11 canteen   12 cheap   13/14 door/dear   15 poor   16 friend   17 aunt   18 restaurant   19 thief   20 great   21 cupboard   22 of course   23 dream   24 favourite   25 group   26 green   27 hour   28 house   29 quiet   30 laugh   31/32 meat/meet   33 beach   34 room   35 again   36/37 food/feed   38 chair   39/40 eat/out

Unit 8 1 ▶ **Play – do – go**
At English schools <u>pupils</u> can <u>play</u> football, <u>hockey</u>/… and <u>volleyball</u>/… . The children can <u>do</u> drama and <u>judo</u>/…, too. In the summer kids <u>go</u> swimming or <u>fishing</u>/… . At the weekend many English children <u>go</u> <u>dancing</u> at a disco.
At German schools we can <u>play …, do …, go …</u> .

2 ▶ **Opposites – a crossword puzzle**
Across: 5 daughter   6 sister   7 downstairs   8 married   9 walk   10 good
Down: 1 *his*   2 dog   3 answer   4 girlfriend   6 in front of   7 over   11 pm

3 ▶ **Word mix**
Do your parents drive you to school? • There's so much traffic here in the morning. • We always go on holiday in the summer. • Has Sita got any plans for next week? • There's a message for you from your mum. • I'm not going to invite Miss Hunt to my party.

4 ▶ **Sound check**
[dʒ]   giraffe, orange, gym, sandwich, judo, large, vegetarian, budgie, message
[ʃ]   shout, delcious, lunch, fashion, Turkish, finished, sheep, beach

5 ▶ **Which words go together?**
clean the bathroom; make invitation cards; have a party; work in the kitchen; act in a play; wait in the car; collect words; carry the shopping bag; want a new dress; drive a bus

6 ▶ **So many 'tos'**
1 *an*   2 vor   3 in   4 bis   5 nach   6 mit   7 in(s)   8 bis

7 ▶ **Odd word out**
1 sandals   2 chips   3 CD shop   4 lion   5 France   6 but   7 country   8 calendar

8 ▶ **Puzzle it out**
today; record; uncle; nothing; December; letter; exercises